THE VIRGINIA HOUSE

A Home For Three Hundred Years

by

Anne M. Faulconer

with photographs by the author

Schiffer Publishing Ltd

Box E, Exton, Pennsylvania 19341

Copyright 1984 © by Anne M. Faulconer.
Library of Congress Catalog Number: 83–51774.

Designed by Ellen J. Taylor

Printed in the United States of America.
ISBN: 0-88740-004-3
Published by Schiffer Publishing Limited
Box E
Exton, Pennsylvania 19341

This book may be purchased from the publisher.
Please include $1.50 postage.
Try your bookstore first.

To my parents

Virginia Davis Faulconer

and

Robert Jamieson Faulconer

Acknowledgments

I am deeply indebted to the staff of the Virginia Historic Landmarks Commission. Without their painstaking research and assistance to me this book could not have been written. I have also made extensive use of Thomas T. Waterman's *The Mansions of Virginia 1706-1776* (New York: Bonanza Books, 1945), and referred occasionally to Emily Ferguson Farrar's two classics *Old Virginia Houses: The Mobjack Country* and *Along the James,* published as one volume by Bonanza Books in 1955.

I thank Rosemary Arneson at the Virginia State Library for her thoughtful assistance. I thank the following owners or their representatives who gave of their time to show me their houses: Mr. and Mrs. Benjamin O. Atkinson, Jr.; The Honorable Edward L. Breeden, Jr. and Mrs. Breeden; Mr. and Mrs. Erwin Campbell; Mr. and Mrs. C. Hill Carter, Jr.; Mrs. J.W.C. Catlett; Mr. J.W.C. Catlett, Jr.; Mr. William Catlett; Mr. and Mrs. William B. Copeland; The Honorable Robert W. Daniel, Jr. and Mrs. Daniel; Miss Marjorie S. Eastwick; Mr. and Mrs. Donald Elmore; Mr. and Mrs. Frederick S. Fisher; Miss Edith Garrison; Mrs. Lester Gayle; Mr. and Mrs. Roger Gregory, Jr.; Dr. and Mrs. Thomas A. Graves, Jr.; Mr. and Mrs. H. Harling; Mr. and Mrs. E.E. Harrison, Jr.; Mrs. Pinckney Harrison; Mr. Carlton Hickman; Mr. and Mrs. Malcolm Jamieson; and Dr. Janet Kimbrough.

Also: Mr. Edgar R. Lafferty, Jr.; Mr. Edgar R. Lafferty, III; Mr. and Mrs. Claude O. Lanciano, Jr.; The Honorable Lewis A. McMurran and Mrs. McMurran; Mrs. Walter O. Major; Mrs. Ludwell Lee Montague; Mr. Cecil G. Moore; Mrs. Charles Beatty Moore; Miss Elizabeth R. Palmer; Mr. and Mrs. B.A. Rennolds; Mr. John H. Richard; Mr. and Mrs. William W. Richardson, III; Dr. Hans Rinecker; Dr. and Mrs. Albert Roper; Mrs. Conway Sheild, Jr.; Mr. and Mrs. McDonald Lee Stephens; Mr. Dan Sydow; Mr. and Mrs. Addison Baker Thompson; Mr. and Mrs. J. Hoge Tyler; Ms. Rosa Washington; Mr. and Mrs. Frank Warrington; Mr. and Mrs. R. Carter Wellford; Mr. and Mrs. James P. Wells; Mr. and Mrs. John Wycoff; and Mr. and Mrs. Ashton Yates.

Thanks are also due to my grandparents, Mr. and Mrs. Robert H. Faulconer, and to Mrs. Landon Carter Catlett, Mr. V. Thomas Forehand, and Miss Anne Dobie Peebles.

Finally I should like to thank Natalie Parnass and her staff, especially Rita Dolphin, for typing the manuscript.

Table of Contents

Introduction

From the 1607 landing at Jamestown, Virginia has occupied a unique place in American history. Its colonial system of government molded superbly practical leaders of men who played a major role in orchestrating the American Revolution and in shaping the policies of the youthful United States. As one of the cornerstones of this system was that leaders should also be gentlemen, the story of Virginia is shot through with a strain of romanticism, a vision of the good life, which is especially attractive to a nostalgic twentieth century.

The seats of power in eighteenth century Virginia were the large plantation houses such as Shirley or Elsing Green which sat at the heart of estates numbering acres in the hundreds of thousands. The plantation masters learned early to wed style with necessity. The skillful design and symmetrical positioning of even such mundane buildings as the kitchen or laundry comprised a formal composition in which a sense of order was paramount. Such order on the brink of what still remained a wild and hostile continent enhanced the prestige of the owner and added to his power.

The love of order sifted down from the very top; because of the constant aspiration toward refinement so prevalent in Virginia life even the humblest farmhouse of this period has touches of grandeur. It is larger in manner than in actual size. The carvers, carpenters, masons, painters and plasterers who plied their trade at Shirley and Elsing Green spent a lifetime working on other, smaller houses and on their own. Their legacy is everywhere to be seen in the numerous pre-nineteenth century houses which have survived, the greatest concentration of which are in the Tidewater area. These buildings, often neglected in the past, are being resurrected as the dream houses of a twentieth century which cherishes the individuality and fine workmanship which went into their creation. They are small enough to be affordable yet have enough history attached to provide inspiration for the restoration enthusiast.

When building his house, each colonial Virginian adapted the prevalent style to what suited his individual needs and preferences so that he could live in the house as comfortably as possible. The houses portrayed in this book were above all, homes.

That every house in this book is lived in today (or being restored so that it can be lived in) is a testament to its durability and adaptability. These houses are survivors. Much about their building dates remains a matter of conjecture due to the almost universal loss of city and county records during the War Between the States. That is an indirect depredation of war; most of these houses have

suffered directly as well. They have been taken over by both hostile and friendly troops during the Revolutionary and Civil Wars and served as headquarters, hospitals, commissaries. In times of peace, their owners have brought them up to date according to the current dictates of fashion. Thus windows have been enlarged, partitions put up, roofs altered, porches added and torn down. What all these houses from large to small have in common is their adaptability, their containing something which every generation to inhabit them has found pleasing.

"Why not tear it down and build something new?" Many of these homes had a narrow escape from the demolisher's hammer, but there was always something about each which made someone reflect (in the words of one current owner) "It was just too good to tear down." The early builders had better materials than we do, which can never be reproduced. They had better timber, cut from trees whose size we cannot imagine today, trees the size of the old tree at The Rowe. There were whole forests of walnut and pine to turn into forty-foot planks and beams a foot square (as at Criss Cross) and with which to panel whole rooms. They had more craftsmen with more time spent in carving the panelling. No wonder their work is so treasured today. It is irreplaceable.

The flexibility offered by the typical Virginia house plan of this period also appeals to the twentieth century. This plan consists of a square or rectangular central house flanked by two smaller dependencies on either side, either connected as wings or separate but equidistant from the main house. The other outbuildings such as the kitchen, dairy, icehouse, dovecote and stable clustered around this central arrangement much as a small village surrounds its church and town hall. This style was followed everywhere, as much as the owner could afford.

Where the outbuildings have survived, the new owner can turn an old barn into a pool house or studio or garage, or he can choose to join it to the main house. There is no contradiction in adapting these buildings to a twentieth century lifestyle while retaining on the outside the authentic flavor of the eighteenth. A dark cellar becomes a modern den or study. The wasted space so common in old houses becomes a typing room under the stairs, storage and closet space, or a convenient nook for books. What the house has been determines what it is today, but does not limit the possibilities called forth by the current owner's needs, just as its builders shaped it to suit their own. Above all, the houses profiled here have endured, and now once again, they flourish.

ADAM KEELING HOUSE

The Adam Keeling House was built between 1683 and 1690 by Thomas Keeling II, whose grandfather arrived in Virginia in 1635, on land left him by his father, Adam Keeling. The Keelings were large landowners in the Virginia Beach area for over two hundred years. The Keeling House was sold by the family in 1881.

The house is now both the oldest owner-occupied house in Virginia, and the oldest house in Virginia to be continuously inhabited. It is notable for the master craftsmanship of its brickwork, Flemish bond with glazed blue headers throughout. In the gables the headers form an inverted chevron pattern which follows the lines of the sharply pitched roof (Sheet 1). This design is possible because the two chimneys are placed inside the walls, a most unusual feature for this period. On both the first and second floors on either side of each chimney is a small closet with a tiny outside window (Sheet 2). While legend has it that from here the musket bearer could shoot while remaining protected from hostile bows and arrows, it is more likely that these closets were used as larders. Their presence makes the Keeling House one of the few old Virginia houses where the twentieth century owners did not have to construct all of the closets themselves (Sheet 3). The distinctive staircase is original (Sheet 4), as is the wall of pine panelling in the living room (Sheet 5). The original south door, worn thin by constant use, now leads to a frame extension added in the 1950's. The west door (Sheet 6) still shows the original brickwork.

Unusual chevron-pattern brickwork

Adam Keeling House, east front

Original closets in second floor bedroom

South door

Panelled north end of living room

West door

Bayville's pastoral setting

BAYVILLE

The spacious farmhouse Bayville was built in 1827 by Peter Singleton II on land originally owned by his mother's family, the Thoroughgoods. Blessed with lovely views, the house faces northeast on Pleasure House Creek, which empties into Lynnhaven Bay. The southwest and formerly main entrance looks down a long lane bordered by giant boxwood.

The chimney ends are enclosed and the brickwork contains a gable window at each end. Forty-seven feet long by thirty feet wide, Bayville is constructed on the center hall plan with two rooms opening either side of the staircase hall with its simple yet distinguished arch. The downstairs rooms retain their original mantels. The two porches were added in 1919 by the current owner's father. Although the original outbuildings have been demolished, the guest house built in 1974 is in keeping with the period of the house.

Enclosed chimney end with gable window

An elegant farmhouse

Rear of house reveals side additions

Bayville's center hall boasts a stately arch

Fine mantel of the Federal period

↑ *Inviting period style guest house* ↓

↑ *Porticoed porches added in 1919 embellish front and rear of
Bayville*

WOODHOUSE-HICKMAN HOUSE

Built in 1830 by the Woodhouse family, who built two other houses nearby, this sturdy brick house was originally a tavern, which explains its position close by the side of the road.

The Great Room of the tavern on the first floor was partitioned later in the nineteenth century into two rooms, now used as a living room and a study, each of which retains the simply carved mantel formerly standing at either end of the original large room. The thick pine flooring used throughout has mellowed to a deep golden brown which never needs polishing. These planks also cover the walls and ceilings of the two attic bedrooms.

The house is noteworthy for its large cluster of outbuildings. In keeping with the early nineteenth century character of the house, the current owner has reconstructed a well cover, woodshed, small barn, ice house, dovecote (which contains the filter pump for a small ornamental pond), chickenhouse, and is at work on a reconstruction of the original outside kitchen which had to be demolished soon after he bought the house. Doing all the work himself, he has made many trips to Colonial Williamsburg to study outbuildings. An eighteenth century visitor to a Tidewater plantation remarked that "when I reached his place, I thought I was entering a rather large village, but later on was told that all of it belonged to him." The owner of the Woodhouse-Hickman House has successfully captured this village atmosphere on a smaller scale.

Nineteenth century tavern transformed into residence

Outbuildings

Pine staircase has mellowed to a deep golden brown

14

Original tavern "Great Room" mantel now main focus of living room

Attic bedroom

Woodshed

Ice house

Chickenhouse

Dovecote

THE ALLMAND-ARCHER HOUSE

Situated on a busy street in downtown Norfolk, the Allmand-Archer House was built during the 1790's and bought in 1802 by Harrison Allmand, a merchant known as "Old Gold Dust" because of his wealth. During the War of 1812 it served as headquarters for American officers, and Lafayette dined here during a reunion of officers of the Revolutionary War. In 1978 the current owner bought the house from a descendant of Harrison Allmand and began his well-documented restoration.

He found the house badly deteriorated. The exterior stucco had fallen off in many places and the chimneys were in danger of toppling. The walls of the house were buckling outward; to counteract this, steel plates were inserted under the brickwork at the four corners of each level. Heavy wires were attached to these plates and tightened to pull the walls back together, "like wrapping a package," the owner notes.

Replastering was necessary throughout the house. The electricity consisted of six crude outlets and the only heat was from coal stoves in the fireplaces. A primitive bathroom had been installed on the third floor in the 1890's; the owner modernized it and constructed another on the second floor. Not wanting to lose the light from its window, in a novel arrangement the owner had the bathroom fixtures placed behind doors which can be pulled shut so that the bathroom door into the hall can be left open at any time.

A landing window between the second and third floors floods the stairway with light. The gradual widening of the angles of the staircase as it ascends gives a light airy feeling to the center of the house. There is a hand-carved bracket beneath each stair.

Dirt and rubbish had accumulated in the basement to a depth of four feet. The current owner excavated it and what used to be wasted space is now a semi-modern study and bar.

One benefit of the previous lack of restoration lay in the wealth of original materials the current owner was able to incorporate into his restoration. Fine old brass locks are used throughout the house. The gas lamp which formerly lit the parlor has been converted to electrical use and now hangs from the ceiling at the very top of the house. Sometime in the nineteenth century a young lady covered the inside of her wardrobe door with fashion plate illustrations cut from magazines, many of which she colored herself. The current owner liked the effect so much that he used the wardrobe doors as doors to a built in closet he added on the third floor. And "Old Gold Dust's" household ledger, in which the week by week expenditure of every penny is set down, still sits on his desk in the parlor.

The Allmand-Archer House lends period charm to a busy modern street

Straightening exterior walls (restoration detail)

17

Center hall before and after replastering (restoration detail)

Hidden bathroom fixtures (restoration detail)

Unusual widening staircase

Stair brackets

Old brass lock

Two details of watercolors found by current owner

Old wardrobe doors adapted to fit modern built-in closet

19 *Meticulous bookkeeping of the past—Harrison Allmand's household ledger*

BOUSH-TAZEWELL HOUSE

The Boush-Tazewell House, built for John Boush, the grandson of Samuel Boush, first mayor of Norfolk, and later mayor himself, originally stood in downtown Norfolk overlooking the harbor. Boush's house was the first important private residence constructed in the city since its destruction by British bombardment during the Revolution. The current owner believes that work on the house was begun in 1779 and finished by 1783.

It remained in the Boush family until it was acquired in 1810 by Littleton Waller Tazewell, U.S. Senator from Virginia from 1824 to 1832 and Governor of Virginia from 1834. His Norfolk house was visited by Lafayette, Henry Clay, John Tyler, and Andrew Jackson. The current owner points out the similarity between the double porticoes of the altered Tazewell Hall in Williamsburg, Tazewell's birthplace and that of the Boush-Tazewell House.

In 1894 the current owner's grandparents bought the house and decided to move it as the neighborhood was becoming too commercialized to be desirable as a residential area. In 1898 the house was carefully dismantled and re-erected on its present site some three miles to the north, at the mouth of the Lafayette River.

The house was not altered by the move and retains today the many features which made it noteworthy. These include the early use of the two-level pedimented portico supported by slender Tuscan columns on the river front, and the dwarf pedimented portico sheltering the land side entrance. Both porticoes are ornamented with modillion cornices. The two story wings at either side of the main block are said to be a later addition.

The main house is constructed on the center hall plan with the hall flanked by pairs of rooms. On the north side, the library and the dining room are divided by a beautifully carved wide elliptical arch, with the original folding doors intact, pegged for easy removal during the summer months. The library bookcases, originally located in an outbuilding when the house stood downtown, were placed here when it was moved.

Another elliptical arch dominates the central hall, a reconstruction made during the current owner's restoration. The stair retains its original stepped base and column balusters. The handrail at the base of the stair was added when the house was moved and this one piece was found to be missing. The floors are all original, except in the dining room where a later floor has been laid atop the wide boards of the earlier floor. The second floor plan largely repeats that of the first, with a narrower arch.

The current owner began her restoration in 1970. As in all old houses, finding space for closets was difficult. The owner notes that space was found here by recessing some of the house's nine fireplaces and by adding on to the back of the upstairs arch.

The Boush-Tazewell House, an early example of historic preservation

Boush-Tazewell House before removal to its present site

Library bookcases

Dwarf pedimented portico formalizes land side of house

Wide arch enhances spaciousness of living and dining rooms

Arch with doors in place

Staircase

Second floor arch

Additional storage space added behind second floor arch

THE SELDEN HOUSE

The Selden House, one of the few remaining Federal houses in Norfolk, was built *circa* 1805 as a country house by Dr. William Boswell Selden on what was then a point of land between a creek and the Elizabeth River. The creek has been filled in and cobblestoned Freemason Street now runs beside the north side of the house.

The house served as Union headquarters in Norfolk during the Civil War; among the officers stationed there was Brig. Gen. Egbert Viele, a civil engineer who laid out New York's Central Park. What is now the wine cellar was used as a Federal prison. Gen. Robert E. Lee stayed here in 1870, his last trip to Norfolk. In the garden, there still stands a gnarled old camellia bush, the first camellia brought to Norfolk from South Carolina. It wintered under glass until the Civil War, when no glass was available, and it was discovered that the plant was hardy enough to withstand the Norfolk winter climate.

It is thought that the two unusual three-sided dormers were added during the mid-nineteenth century to gain increased living space by using the third floor attic. In the last quarter of the nineteenth century a two-story Georgian revival porch was placed at the south end of the house and Victorian "gingerbreading" added to the exterior woodwork. Both porch and gingerbread have since disappeared.

Selden descendants lived here until 1955. The house then stood vacant until the Chrysler Museum rented it in 1961 for use as an art school. In 1973, it was severely damaged by fire, and was put up for sale to a buyer who would restore it.

The current owners declared that it was to be a home, rather than a museum. While deciding against a strictly period restoration, they assembled a fine team of craftsmen to rebuild and restore such details as the parquet flooring in the hall charred by the fire and the staircase. New balusters were carved to match the old. New mantels were carefully copied from old ones of the Federal period, down to the last detail of carving. The two sets of double doors on either side of the house which divide the living room from the family room and library from the dining room were carefully restored where fire had eaten through. The effect of the owners' painstaking efforts is that of an old house happily lived in continuously, rather than interrupted by the vicissitudes of vacancy and fire.

The Selden House, one of the few surviving Federal Houses in Norfolk

23 *Rear view of the Selden House at the turn of the century*

Selden House before twentieth-century restoration

Restored parquet flooring

Reconstructed staircase

24

Carefully matched balusters

Meticulously copied period-style mantels

Detail of mantel carving

Restored double doors

"A VIRGINIA HOUSE"

This house was built by Thurmer Hoggard *circa* 1760 on the banks on Broad Creek overlooking the Elizabeth River. It remained in the Hoggard family until 1952.

The original main block of the house measures 50 by 27 feet and the brickwork is Flemish bond. The central hall runs straight through the house in the plan often followed in Virginia to conduct cooling breezes off the water during the hot summer. To counteract the opposite effect in winter, the rooms on the land front facing northeast have only one window per room, while those facing southwest have two. This practical but unusual arrangement gives the house the appearance of two quite different houses, depending on which side one observes. Each is perfectly balanced; the river front has a row of five windows at second floor level balancing a row of two windows, porch and two windows on the first floor, while the land front has three windows on the second floor and one window, porch and the other window on the first floor.

The living room boasts a heart pine floor with no cut; all boards are the full twenty-foot width of the room. The deeply recessed windows retain their handmade panes of glass. All mantels in the central portion of the house are original. Many years ago the second bedroom upstairs was divided into a bedroom and study, each with its own fireplace. There was only room to squeeze in a little half-door between the division and the staircase.

The brick dining room addition dates to *circa* 1860. Evidently it was added on first and when the door was cut through it was found that the floors did not quite meet; there was one and a half inches difference between them. The modern kitchen was added in 1954. The fine porches are crowned with pediments and exhibit Chippendale trellis work. A few steps from the house lies the old clapboard kitchen flanked by brick dairy and clapboard smokehouse, a remarkable preservation of the original "plantation street". (Owner wishes house to remain anonymous).

Chippendale trellis porch

1860 brick dining room flanked by main house and modern frame kitchen

River front

Street of plantation outbuildings

PEMBROKE

Pembroke lies at the end of a long lane, on the banks of the Nansemond River. Built in 1701, the house is a transitional combination of the picturesque gables of the seventeenth century and the symmetry characteristic of the eighteenth. Like the much larger Elsing Green, Pembroke is U-shaped, but its small size and the number of its gables and dormers give it a charming picturesque quality not found in strictly classical architecture. Its style is lively from any angle.

According to tradition the builder was an English sea captain, Captain Jack, and the house was named for the Earl of Pembroke. The destruction of the Colonial records makes it impossible to check the house's origins more thoroughly. A British sympathizer, Captain Jack quit the colonies abruptly at the beginning of the Revolution, leaving his overseer, Patrick Wilkinson, in charge of the plantation. The current owners bought Pembroke around 1945 for its two hundred acres of farmland. They were not aware of the house's historical value until they received a letter in 1950 from Harold Ickes, then Secretary of the Interior, advising them that the house was worthy of careful preservation for future generations. They decided to restore the house with the help of an architect who had worked with Colonial Williamsburg. The major work of restoration was carried out between 1950 and 1952.

The original brick walls, laid in Flemish bond, were as solid as ever, but much needed to be rebuilt inside. The architect advised against the addition of the screen porch overlooking the river as not being of the period. The owners, however, wished to make use of the river view and have never regretted the addition.

Pembroke, side view

Pembroke from southwest

Pembroke, a charming study in gables and dormers

Screen porch added by current owners affords a lovely river view

29

JOSEPH JORDAN HOUSE

During the early eighteenth century, the planters who settled in the Blackwater River area south of the James River tended to be poorer than those who settled nearer the James. It is now believed, however, that around the time of the Revolution, these men underwent a dramatic upswing in their fortunes. This economic change is attested to by a group of small but substantial houses built at this time, of which the Joseph Jordan House is the largest. The small brick and frame farmhouse was built in 1795 as the homestead for Joseph Jordan's 1900 acres. The original structure is a story and a half with brick ends. The bricks are laid in Flemish bond with a single glazed chevron pattern following the rise of the gable. The clerestory windows running most of the length of the house were probably added between 1820 and 1840. They are an interesting intermediate step between a half-story with dormers and a full second story. Before their addition, the only light to the upper part of the house came from the pair of tiny windows in each gable. The current owner states that the original clapboard roof which covers the original house remains beneath the shingle roof. This is one of only nine known examples of a clapboard roof surviving in Virginia; another is at Kempsville. The two-story frame addition at the north end was built somewhat later than the main house, as was the kitchen extending to the rear, now a parlor.

The current owner bought the Joseph Jordan House in 1978 and decided that it was "too good to tear down; there was enough old timber in it for three modern houses." During restoration he added the porch on the rear ell. The carved wooden ornamentation to the front porch was copied from that on an old schoolhouse nearby.

Side view

Joseph Jordan House, rear view showing modern living room addition

Joseph Jordan House, original structure

WOLFTRAP FARM

Wolftrap Farm was built between 1810 and 1820 by Wilson Jones and is today the home of his great-great-granddaughter. The house is unique in being the only known dwelling in Virginia with a double tier of dormers. The porch was recently enclosed.

Double-dormered Wolftrap Farm

Wolftrap Farm following porch enclosure

31

BRANDON

Brandon, one of Virginia's great plantation houses, sits today in 4500 acres of woodlands, pastures and gardens, not much diminished from the original Brandon land grant of 5,000 acres patented in 1616. The farm, in continuous operation since that time, is the oldest agricultural enterprise in the United States.

Lack of proper documentation makes it difficult to date the different structures at Brandon. No doubt the earliest is the brick blockhouse designed for defense against Indian raids which has been thought to date from the time of Richard Quiney, who bought the plantation in 1635. (Richard Quiney's brother Thomas was married to William Shakespeare's daughter Judith.) Located to the west of the main house, this one story brick building is laid in Flemish bond. The door and shutters are covered in the original iron.

The house itself is a long seven part brick structure consisting of a two-story central block, flanked by one-story wings, each of which is linked to a two-story dependency by a low one-story hyphen. The pyramid roof capped by a carved pineapple is reminiscent of that of Battersea with its acorn. It is believed that Nathaniel Harrison II built the dependencies first, and added the central portion, based on a design from Robert Morris' *Select Architecture,* after 1757 when the book was published. Like the other 'long' houses Battersea and Tazewell Hall, a Jeffersonian connection is claimed for Brandon's design; it is known that Jefferson owned a copy of Morris' book. From the exterior there is indeed a marked similarity between Brandon's central portion and that of Tazewell Hall.

The center hall was altered in the early nineteenth century, when the triple arch Ionic screen and present staircase were installed. It is thought that the original hall may have been divided into a stair hall with a salon as at Battersea. During the Civil War Federal troops fired on the house, ripped out the interior panelling and burned the plantation outbuildings.

Renovation began in 1926 at which time the panelling was restored. The pedimented chimney piece in the drawing room also needed extensive alteration. The massive original kitchen fireplace still stands in the east wing. The central hall of the west wing contains a fine original Chippendale trellis staircase and four panelled rooms of the same period and style as the main part of the house on a smaller scale. On the west side of this wing a modern addition accommodates necessary bathrooms.

Seventeenth century blockhouse, a fortress against Indian raids

Brandon land front

32   *Restored drawing room chimney piece*

Majestic main hall

Brandon central block

Watercolor of Brandon during Civil War

Chinese Chippendale staircase

Original kitchen fireplace still in constant use

Guest room chimney piece

BATTERSEA

Battersea (Sheet 7) was built between 1765 and 1770 for Colonel John Banister, a leading citizen of Virginia and of the young United States. A close friend of Thomas Jefferson, Col. Banister was a member of the Virginia House of Burgesses and the Continental Congress. He also served as the first mayor of Petersburg. On visiting Battersea in 1781 the Marquis de Chastellux noted that "Mr. Banister's handsome country house…is really worth seeing. It is decorated rather in the Italian, than the English or American style, having three porticoes at the three principal entries…" The effect today is even more Italianate than it was originally, as the original Flemish bond brickwork was stuccoed in the early nineteenth century, at which time the broad arched front door was also added. (Sheet 8) The porch was altered between 1840 and 1850. The end porticoes were only recently enclosed. The original Chippendale trellis stair is considered the finest in Virginia (Sheet 9). What is now the kitchen and was probably the former dining room retains its original doors and trim. The old kitchen with its massive fireplaces still stands at the rear of the house.

The plan of Battersea (Sheets 10, 11, 12) shows similarities to those of Brandon and Tazewell Hall. Circumstantial evidence such as Col. Banister's friendship with Jefferson points to Jefferson having a hand in the design, but the connection has never been authenticated.

Chippendale trellis staircase, finest of its kind in Virginia

Battersea's windows show Italian influence

Original panelled west door

Glassed-in portico, a modern addition

Old kitchen

TAZEWELL HALL

Once a Williamsburg town house, Tazewell Hall now sits on a quiet pine wooded site on the banks of the James River in Newport News. The house's journey and the alterations it has undergone make an interesting story.

The house has been restored to its original appearance. The Architectural Department of Colonial Williamsburg has determined that Tazewell Hall and its dependencies once occupied a position of importance in the Williamsburg town plan, along with the Capitol, the Palace, and the Wren Building. Although an exact date of construction has not been established, it is believed that Sir John Randolph built the house around 1730.

It is also noteworthy that Sir John was a friend of Thomas Jefferson, and that Tazewell Hall's design bears a close resemblance to other Jeffersonian-linked houses such as Brandon and Battersea. In the original plan the central hall was two stories high, as it is today, with a pilastered side wall. The height and the many windows give this hall a great sense of light and air. The current owner states that on a snowy moonlit night one can read here, so great is the reflection. The openings to the passages are decorated with tall arches and there are arches on either side of the fireplace in the drawing room.

The house was bought by John Tazewell in 1778. An 1836 insurance policy describes the detachment of one wing and its relocation nearby, while the other wing was removed. The central portion was rebuilt as a two-story structure. A staircase was installed in the center hall.

In 1908 the main portion alone was moved from its original location at the foot of South England Street to the side of the street to make way for a real estate development. During the restoration of Colonial Williamsburg the entire house was dismantled and removed to a warehouse until it was bought by the current owners and moved to its present site in 1954. In rebuilding, they followed the eighteenth century floor plan as closely as possible, while allowing for the addition of closets, baths and a kitchen. To accommodate these twentieth century conveniences the house is now four feet wider than it was in the eighteenth century. The terminal wings were rebuilt and the halls in the connecting wings are narrower to allow space for bedrooms. A formal garden leads from the house to the river bank. A modern outbuilding is in keeping with the period of the house.

Tazewell Hall in its new location on the James River

Light and airy central hall

Tazewell Hall from the southwest

Formal garden

Modern outbuilding modelled after eighteenth century smokehouse

Corner of central hall

Central portion showing similarity to central portion of Brandon

PRESIDENT'S HOUSE,
COLLEGE OF WILLIAM AND MARY

The President's House at the College of William and Mary is the oldest home of a college or university president in continuous use in America. It was built in 1732 by Henry Cary, Jr., a former student of the college. In 1781 Lord Cornwallis commandeered the house for use as his headquarters. He evicted the President, James Madison, (cousin of the future U.S. President) and refused to allow him to draw water from his own well. Shortly afterward, a fire occurred during the use of the house as a hospital for French officers. A generous Louis XVI authorized the French treasury to cover the cost of repairing the damage.

Throughout its history the President's House has been host to both national and international leaders from George Washington and Thomas Jefferson to the Marquis de Lafayette, Queen Elizabeth II and Winston Churchill. The Prince of Wales visited here in 1981.

The house is a model of the early Georgian style in Eastern Virginia. The fine Flemish bond brickwork is noteworthy. The detail of the basement entrance gives a

The President's House, College of William and Mary, a model of the Virginia early Georgian style

closeup of the pattern, with the headers covered in a silver gray glaze. The entrance on either side is crowned with a simple pediment. In the garden stands the wooden kitchen of 1817, now used as a guest house.

The house underwent a major renovation in 1928 through 1932 as part of the restoration of Colonial Williamsburg. During this time features added after the eighteenth century were removed and the exterior restored to its original appearance. In 1977 the current President, Dr. Thomas A. Graves, Jr., enlisted the aid of Clement E. Conger, curator of the White House, as Chairman of the Program to Furnish the President's House. Feeling that the President's House is the most important brick house in Williamsburg, Conger and his committee began to acquire by loan and donation a collection of eighteenth century furniture equal in quality to the house's fine collection of early portraits. An arch was recently added between the parlors to open up the rooms and to add to the grandeur imparted by the new furnishings. The second floor is lived in comfortably by the President's family with their own furnishings, while the third, formerly an attic, is now used as a modern family room and study.

President's House and garden

Striking Flemish bond brickwork

Pediment atop entrance, typical of house's fine simplicity

Frame kitchen, now a guest house, behind garden well

*Portrait of John Page of Rosewell
1744-1808*

Staircase and central hall

Arch between parlors is a recent addition

42

ST. GEORGE TUCKER HOUSE

The St. George Tucker House was built soon after 1788 by the eminent jurist St. George Tucker, friend of Thomas Jefferson and the first law professor at William and Mary College. At the time of building an earlier, simpler structure was incorporated into the design; the windows and exterior clapboard walls of this 1720's house are still visible from three rooms on the ground floor.

The house has been added to many times and its rambling nature is more readily apparent from the back than the front. The entire house is 128 feet long. It is divided into five distinct parts. The main section in which the earlier two-up and two-down structure is preserved, is enclosed by large end chimneys, beyond which a one and a half story wing projects on either side east and west. A small one-story passageway connects the old kitchen with the west wing. The original massive kitchen chimneys are still functional. The roof and shutters have been restored to the color specified by St. George Tucker: "brown with enough red lead to give it spirit".

A small porch at the main front entrance leads to the center hall. The arch here was added by Colonial Williamsburg. The large rear parlor is noteworthy for its double stairs, one staircase being located at either end of the room. The east is the elder, built by St. George Tucker in 1788. The west was added by one of his nineteenth century descendants.

View of hallway with former exterior door and wall

St. George Tucker House

Note series of additions

"Enough red lead to give it spirit"

Hall arch added by Colonial Williamsburg restoration

Original kitchen

East and west main staircases

THE SHEILD HOUSE

The Sheild House at the corner of Main and Nelson Streets in Yorktown was built in 1699 by Thomas Sessions, a merchant. In 1862 it was the headquarters of one of McClellan's generals during the invasion and occupation of the Peninsula by Federal troops.

Despite its small size, the Sheild House is massively built with thick, substantial chimneys (Sheets 13 & 14). The clipped-end gables (Sheet 15) are echoed in the construction of the dormers; the second story is lit by gable windows as well as the dormers. The house is two stories high above a full basement (Sheets 16, 17, 18).

The front door is unusually large. The center hall is dominated by a carved wooden arch very grand for its time, indicative of the eighteenth century and the transitional period of the house (Sheet 19). The staircase, however, tucked in a small passage opening off the dining room is simple and unadorned. Throughout the house the doors are hand carved, resulting in slightly irregular panelling. The flooring of the hall and parlor is of one cut pine, consisting only of boards long enough to run the width of the room, in this case, ten and a half feet.

The small but solidly built Sheild House

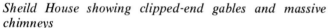

Sheild House showing clipped-end gables and massive chimneys

Grand carved wooden arch

Staircase hall

Unassuming main staircase

Panelled door

47

BELLE AIR

Belle Air's current owner notes that "Belle Air is the oldest frame house in Virginia and the only surviving southern example of a seventeenth century frame house". The origins of the property have been traced back to Colonel Thomas Stegge II, great-uncle of William Byrd II, the builder of Westover. The present house is located on the highest point of land of Colonel Stegge's 1700 acres. The destruction of the Charles City County colonial records makes it difficult to determine whether this is the house begun by Colonel Stegge in 1655 or one built by Lieutenant Colonel Daniel Clarke in 1662 on land bought from Colonel Stegge.

What is known is that the house, so unpretentious in size according to twentieth century standards, was a fine plantation dwelling in the seventeenth. The care lavished on its interior architectural features show that Belle Air was the home of a gentleman of taste and consequence. In the exposed framing, the beams served as both structure and trim. The timber used in the distinctive exposed framing of the interior was heart of pine, the core of trees at least eight feet in diameter. These huge timbers were joined into the chimneys, the main supports of the house. Belle Air's current owner observes that "if the chimney were not well built, then the beams caught fire. A dozen or so northern examples of these homes have survived. They were built of oak and other hardwoods which did not catch fire as easily as the heart of the pine." The exposed frame type of construction exemplified in the seventeenth century portion of Belle Air was forbidden by building ordinances after 1700. The stair has been called "the finest example of Jacobean colonial balustrade work ever recorded in America" and is unusual for its fine carving and closed-string arrangement.

Belle Air's long history is an illustration of the number of alterations old houses undergo during the course of centuries. The seventeenth century eastern portion of the house was originally a one and a half story clipped-end gable roofed structure, with a center passage and a room on either side. During repairs and improvements from 1730 to 1760 the dormers were raised to their present height and the board roof was replaced with shingles. Cupboards were installed in the eastern room downstairs and the window light was installed over the front door. The flooring downstairs was replaced with the present floor; the seventeenth century flooring consisting of planks nearly three inches thick remains upstairs.

The west addition was constructed between 1790 and 1800. At this time the clipped end gables were covered. The western chimney was doubled and became the middle chimney. The top of the east chimney was altered to correspond with the west chimney. The mantel in the east room downstairs was replaced and that in the west room altered to correspond more closely to the new mantel installed in the western addition.

In 1820 a porch was built at the west front entrance to correspond with one added forty years earlier to the east front. In the 1860's the cupboards in the downstairs rooms were torn out by Union troops in search of valuables. Around 1880 the present kitchen was built to the north of the house but not connected to it.

The current owner acquired Belle Air in 1945, at which time the house had stood empty for over twenty-five years. After establishing its significance through research and consultation with Colonial Williamsburg experts, careful repairs and renovations were carried out. The present dining room was built atop the foundation lines of the seventeenth century house-kitchen torn down between 1730 and 1760. The two porches added in 1780 and 1820 were removed, and their massive timber posts were used in the construction of a screened porch at the rear of the house. Closets were installed upstairs and in the master bedroom in the western addition, and bookcases in the library (downstairs east room) to replace the cupboards torn out during the 1860's. The house retains its original plantation features of covered well, detached kitchen and laundry and smokehouse.

The centuries come together in harmony and sit lightly upon Belle Air today. The livable house works together; the eighteenth, nineteenth and twentieth century additions do not detract from the fine interior character of the seventeenth century section. The current owner emphasizes that despite being lavishly furnished with antiques Belle Air is not a museum house, it is a home.

Belle Air

Fine colonial Jacobean staircase

Exposed frame construction is both functional and decorative

49

Note fine staircase details

Window light, an eighteenth century improvement

West addition

First floor bedroom

Screed Park et Column Detail

Screen porch uses timber from previous additions

Belle Air - circa 1880

Porch added 1820

Kitchen and laundry

Second floor bedroom

Smokehouse

Covered well

BERKELEY

Berkeley was built in 1726 by Benjamin Harrison IV. The land had been settled long before that, and was the site of the first official Thanksgiving to take place in the New World in December, 1619. McClellan's troops camped here during the campaign of 1862, and 'Taps' was composed and first played at Berkeley during that time. The builder's son Benjamin Harrison V was a member of the Continental Congress, signer of the Declaration of Independence, and Governor of Virginia. His son William Henry Harrison, President of the United States, was born at Berkeley.

The house, flanked on either side by washed stucco dependencies, is the oldest three-story brick house in Virginia that can prove its date. It is notable as the first use of a heroic pediment roof in Virginia. The lines of the roof are echoed in the basement entrance and in the two main doors, which are modern. The brick work is Flemish bond above the water table and English bond below.

The interior has been altered since 1726. A fire necessitated some rebuilding around 1800, at which time the hall arch was added, and the arched passages between the two east rooms. There has been much speculation as to the original placement of the stair. As it was the usual practice to place the stair in the central hall at this time, some experts believe that in the 1800 alterations the staircase was moved to its present position in the northwest corner of the house behind a false door. The staircase is certainly very simple for a house of Berkeley's stature, but the current owner believes that its location was by original intent so that the central hall could be used as a ballroom without having to pay ballroom taxes. The first floor windows retain their old folding wooden shutters.

Land side

River side

When the current owner settled at Berkeley he planted the willows which now seem so much a part of the house's charm, and added the gazebo between the house and the river. He had to remove three coats of red barn paint from the brickwork and install new window sashes. An interesting touch was the way he left visible the builder's name, written in plaster uncovered during restoration work. Other eighteenth century features he found intact include the thirty-six inch brick pipe in the basement which still ensured good drainage.

The first floor of the house and the gardens are open to the public. The current owner was much touched when one of these visitors remarked that she hoped he was not going to "be disappointed in Paradise after living here."

One of two flanking dependencies

First use of heroic pediment roof in Virginia

Basement entrance

Main door, river side

Hall arch added 1800

Arched passage opens up two east rooms

False door ensures symmetry of center hall

Simple staircase

Wooden shutters add character to a first floor window

Berkeley's gazebo, a favorite site for local weddings

DOGHAM FARM

The plantation of Dogham dates back to 1635 when Joseph Royal received a land grant of eleven hundred acres from the King of England. Opinions vary as to when the oldest part of the white clapboard house was built, some dating it as early as 1652, others much later. The property was occupied by the Royal family until 1928, when it was acquired by the current owner and her late husband. In the 1930's they added a sleeping porch in the rear of the house. In 1941, they added the modern wing with four dormers which stands at a right angle to the older section and is connected to it by a small one-story passageway. The addition, made without the advice of an architect, was one and a half feet too high upon completion; it then had to be lowered to match the height of the old portion of the house. The two now blend very well together. A terrace below the new addition is much used in the summer months. The construction of the new chimney shows some outstanding modern brick work.

Dogham is also noteworthy for its fine old trees.

Modern chimney shows same excellent workmanship as older part of the house

Oldest part of Dogham

Terrace beneath 1941 addition a favorite summer spot

Dogham's ancient trees enhance house's air of antiquity

1941 addition gives Dogham an L-shape

GREENWAY

Greenway is of interest for the unusually complete survival it represents of a small mid-eighteenth century plantation house with its outbuildings intact and in good condition (Sheet 20). President Tyler was born at Greenway in 1790, and lived here from 1821 until 1829.

The one and a half story house (Sheets 21, 22, 23, 24) is also remarkable for its fine interior woodwork. The drawing room contains a fine carved mantel. (Sheet 25) The other rooms also contain noteworthy mantels (Sheets 26, 27, 28, 29) with built in cupboards. The main staircase is unusually simple (Sheet 30). The 1934 HABS surveyors found the original brass and wrought iron fittings of great interest (Sheet 31).

The office, which President Tyler used as his law office, is a few steps west of the house (Sheet 32). The other buildings stand in a short "street" east of the house. These buildings are the old kitchen, the laundry and bakery, and smokehouse. The old outbuildings demonstrate the potential for adaptation which exists in all parts of an old plantation, for each (with the exception of the smokehouse) is now an individual dwelling.

For additional architectural details, see sheets 33 and 34.

Carved mantel graces drawing room

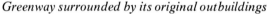

Greenway surrounded by its original outbuildings

Cupboards built into drawing room mantel

President Tyler's law office

Unadorned main staircase

Plantation street

59

Kitchen

Laundry and bakery

Smokehouse

POPLAR SPRINGS

Poplar Springs, a small one and a half story frame house, was built in the mid-eighteenth century. When the current owners bought it in 1938, they demolished the old slave quarters ("the quarterhouse") near the main house. In the 1960's they employed an architect specializing in old houses to design an addition. In 1982 they added a large bedroom and bath to the rear of the house on the first floor, also in keeping with the period of the house.

Poplar Springs retains much of its original thick window glass. The front porch leads to a central hall with a room opening off onto either side. The steep staircase faces the rear of the hall, and beneath it an old door leads to the cellar. When the current owners bought Poplar Springs there were no stairs to the basement, and they were told by an expert that access had originally been by rope ladder.

The cellar door, like the others in the early portion of the house, is a model of eighteenth century door construction. It retains its original wooden latch. The doors leading to the living room and the dining room off the central hall were constructed with wooden pegs rather than nails. From the side one can see how a board was slotted in to form the transverse 'T' on the cross.

Artist's rendition of Poplar Springs with 1960's addition

One and a half story Poplar Springs

Original house and 1960's addition

Rounded boxwood adds to Poplar Springs' eighteenth century ambiance

Steeply angled staircase

Cellar door

Cellar door's original wooden latch

Dining room door, cross and book pattern

Door's wooden peg construction

Slotted door panel

63

THE ROWE

The Rowe, a three-part frame house situated on the banks of the James River, was probably built in two separate stages. The story-and-a-half north wing may have been built by David Minge before his death in 1779, and it is likely that his son George enlarged the house to its present size before his death in 1808.

Today the house consists of a two story central section similar to that of Battersea, Brandon and Tazewell Hall flanked by two-story-and-a-half wings, each with three gabled dormers. The central section is crowned with a pediment and modillion cornice. The central chimney on the land side of the house was enclosed in the mid-nineteenth century by extending the house several feet.

The setting of the house is particularly striking because of the size and number of old trees. The current owner believes that "whoever chose this spot to build their house selected it quite carefully with the three large trees in mind." Until 1927 a huge butternut tree stood close to the house. Thought to be over a thousand years old, this tree was thirty-three to thirty-six feet in circumference and supposedly is the large tree used as a landmark in Captain John Smith's map of Virginia. The early settlers used it as a guide upriver and later on, river pilots used it as a "point." The photograph reproduced is the only one surviving of this tree.

The Rowe's three part structure displays the symmetry so beloved by eighteenth century Virginians

The Rowe

Central section crowned by a weathered but still stately pediment

Ancient butternut tree formerly standing near The Rowe. Note size of man in relation to tree

SHIRLEY

Shirley is an illustration of the effect to which dependencies can be used to create and enhance an effect of great formality and grandeur. The house is approached from the north (land) side through a series of four fine outbuildings symmetrically placed to form a forecourt and avenue of approach to the main house. Each of the forecourt buildings is a study in symmetry itself, such as the west storehouse. The laundry and the kitchen would make admirable houses on their own today. These two buildings, as are the storehouses, are notable for their pediment roofs, similar to the roof at Berkeley. Outside the forecourt the round dovecote stands with the Lombardy poplars lining the drive forming a backdrop.

The main house, identical on both land and river fronts, is noteworthy for many reasons. Its two-story heroic porticoes are emphasized by the plastered and whitened wall behind them. The porticoes add to the stateliness of the view towards the James River. Unlike other Virginia houses of this period it does not have a wide central hall extending from front to back. Here the carved walnut staircase rises for three floors without any visible means of support. This "floating staircase" was constructed on heavy iron bars driven deep into the four foot thick walls of the house.

Opinions differ as to the date of Shirley's construction. One architectural theory has it that the forecourt buildings were built first, *circa* 1740, and that the main house was built in 1769. The current owner believes that both house and dependencies were constructed at the same time, in 1723. The plantation land has passed down through inheritance since Edward Hill patented it in 1660.

West storehouse from the south

Shirley forecourt

West storehouse from west

Note pediment roof of laundry forecourt building

Spacious kitchen larger than many a modern home

Dovecote

James River view

Magnificent porticoes

WESTGARDEN

Built by the Hargrave family in 1737, the current owner believes Westgarden to be the oldest brick house with a gambrel roof in Charles City County. The end chimneys are enclosed. A kitchen addition was made on the west side in 1968 at which time indoor plumbing was added as well, and electricity replaced gaslight. The addition does not detract from the cottage-like appearance of the house.

Westgarden is built on the central hall plan, with two rooms on each floor opening off the hall. The steep staircase, formerly enclosed, was opened and given balusters in the alterations of 1968. The house retains its early mantels.

Westgarden from west

Oldest gambrel roof brick house in Charles City County

Westgarden from east

Formerly enclosed staircase

Original mantel in center hall

70

Staircase ascends at a steep angle

WESTOVER

Westover's builder, William Byrd II, was renowned throughout Virginia for his good taste. Constructed between 1725 and 1730, Westover is a monument to his sense of style.

Set on a smooth bank of the James River near the water's edge, Westover gives an impression immediately of grandeur and immense size. The vast steep hipped roof and tall chimneys carry this impression even further. The tall tulip poplars which in no way dwarf the house have been there since 1787 or earlier. In Byrd's original plan the dependencies were not designed to be linked with the mansion; the simple west dependency of 1709 or earlier forms a contrast to the style of the main house. Its twin on the east, which housed Byrd's famous library, was destroyed by McClellan's troops in 1862. The gambrel-roofed replacement and the arcades linking both were added during the 1920's.

The door over the main entrance on the river (south) front is perhaps the most copied door in America. The north door has also been much reproduced. The pair of wrought iron gates hung on stone columns surmounted by eagles are perhaps the finest example of this sort of work in America. They are in turn part of a clairvoyee, a long screen of ironwork forming a wall. While there are many examples of clairvoyee work on English estates of the period, this is the only known example in America. The clairvoyee is also notable for the series of ten fine stone finials.

The interior follows the central hall plan, although the hall itself is set slightly off center. The two west rooms were turned into one dining room in alterations made during 1900. Along with Shirley, Westover is the only mansion to have a major staircase ascending for three flights. These two are also the only Virginia mansions with attics designed to be used for bedroom space. The hall is graced by a fine plasterwork ceiling.

The black marble mantel in the southeast drawing room is said to have come from William Byrd II's London town house.

South door, possibly the most copied door in America

Westover's imposing design

West dependency built prior to main house

North door

Wrought iron gate, part of clairvoyee

Staircase

Drawing room

73

WOODBURN

John Tyler, tenth President of the United States, built Woodburn around 1815. The house, currently undergoing restoration, is a three part frame structure. Like the Rowe, it consists of a two-story central section flanked by one-story wings. Its front gable-end facade contains a gable window while the back ends in a gable alone. The impression of height is augmented by the tall chimneys.

The interior of Woodburn is distinguished by its elegant woodwork. The stair in the southwest corner of the hall runs across the front of the central block, like that at Shirley diagonally across a front window. Each wing contains a single room. The original smokehouse has recently been restored.

President Tyler described Woodburn as a "decent and comfortable dwelling." During his residence there he served as U.S. Congressman from the district. The house passed out of the Tyler family in 1836 until bought by the current owner, a descendent of President Tyler.

Smokehouse

Woodburn, rear view

74

Woodburn, dwarfed by giant trees

Tall chimneys augment height of roof

CRISS CROSS

According to tradition Criss Cross (also known as Christ's Cross) was built by George Poindexter about 1690. It is believed that the house was used as a commissary during the Civil War. The current owners bought the house in 1953 and restored it to its general original appearance.

The brick house is T-shaped (cross-shaped) in plan (Sheets 35 & 36), and like nearby Foster's Castle, was a one and a half story building with a two-story projection in the center (Sheets 37 & 38), a seventeenth and very early eighteenth century Virginia building form. Nineteenth century alterations replaced the three brick gables with wood and it was decided to keep them this way in the 1953 restoration. The end chimneys date from the nineteenth century, but are close to the design of the original. The back wing is said to have been added in 1790 and raised to two stories in the late nineteenth century. In 1953, it was encased in one story of brick and given a gambrel roof.

The interior of Criss Cross is noteworthy for its seventeenth century structural system and several rare period details. The ceiling of the porch has a large summer beam and exposed framing. An original set of double doors believed to be the oldest wooden doors in America leads from the porch into the hall (Sheet 39). A partition which had converted the original hall and parlor plan to a center hall plan was removed in 1953. Through the ceiling of the hall and dining room runs a large summer beam of heart pine more than twelve inches square and over forty feet long. The beam is supported at the wall between the two rooms by a decorated post. The post is decorated with a unique Jacobean folk carving (Sheet 40).

Double doors from porch entrance showing beamed ceiling

Wooden gables added in nineteenth century

Rear wing

Criss Cross

Rear wing

Double doors from hall

Unique carved summer beam, hall view

Unique beam, dining room view

Detail of Jacobean folk carving

78

FOSTER'S CASTLE

It is believed that Colonel Joseph Foster built Foster's Castle (also called "The Castle") between 1685 and 1690. Like nearby Criss Cross it is a T-shaped brick house originally constructed as one and a half stories with a two-story central porch projection at the front (Sheets 41 & 42). Unlike Criss Cross it retains its nineteenth century raised roof, although the lines on the original structure including the round window in the gable of the porch are clearly visible where the dark red nineteenth century brick meets the original brickwork (Sheets 43 & 44). The colonnaded porch is a later addition. The three small first floor windows which have kept their arched openings are original (Sheet 45). The two porch windows were slightly moved in the 1873 alterations but they are approximately the same size and in the same position as the original windows.

For further architectural details, see sheets 46 and 47.

Side view showing original seventeenth century brickwork

Foster's Castle

Side view

Small seventeenth century window

Detail of porch windows

LAND'S END

Land's End has a distinctly nautical air, a legacy of its builder Captain John Sinclair, who began construction of the house in 1796. The original three-story house built on the center hall plan with two rooms flanking the hall on each floor was completed by 1800. In 1840 a one-story eighteen by twenty-two foot north wing was added to serve as a small ballroom for Captain Sinclair's granddaughters. A short flight of steps connected this wing two feet above ground with the ground floor basement. Renovations in the 1930's raised the roof of the north wing, necessitating the addition of more steps at the second and third levels to maintain ceiling heights. The many steps give a rambling effect to Land's End; part of the charm of the house is the split-level effect so unexpected from a quick glance at the exterior.

When the current owners acquired the house in 1970, they found many of the eighteenth century features intact. The crossbars and iron receivers on the double doors at the front are still used for security. The original lightning rod continues to provide adequate protection from the

Front door retains original crossbars and iron receivers

Land's End

thunderstorms so frequent in the area. The original main staircase is noteworthy for the unusually wide eighteen inch first cut pine panels in the stairwell.

In their restoration the current owners placed all modern conveniences in the 1840 north wing. The dance parlor became the kitchen. A touch of the past was incorporated into the new kitchen fireplace in a hand-adzed white oak beam from one of the outbuildings demolished in 1968. The new housing for the well is in keeping with the period of the original outbuildings. The brick steps connecting the kitchen with the rest of the house are "bullnosed" with a thick pine insert, a technique used in the eighteenth century to soften the impact of bricks on feet. On the third floor wasted space was turned into closets with doors designed to match the original eighteenth century doors. A French drain in the eighteenth century manner was added around the perimeter of the house. The water table extending to seven and a half feet above ground was placed at this height because of the low four-foot site elevation. An outside stairway was attached to the second level portico, thus giving ready access to the garden from two floors.

Eighteenth century lightning rod still protects house from thunderstorms

Modern kitchen fireplace uses antique beam

What appears to be eighteenth century smokehouse is actually modern well

Bullnosed steps

Modern closets make use of wasted space

Water table and French drain

Pine staircase

Outside staircase a modern addition

LITTLE ENGLAND

According to tradition, Little England was built in 1716 by Captain John Perrin, although some architectural opinion places the date in the second half of the eighteenth century. The brick house stands between Sara's Creek and the York River, and overlooks the York. On the river front there are five dormers; on the land side only three. The notable brickwork is of Flemish bond with widely scattered headers. The windows and doors are surmounted by decorative rubbed and gauged splayed arches. A rubbed belt course indicates the second floor level and the two-course water table consists of a concave above a convex molding.

The house was little altered from its construction until 1939. At this time the interior had not been painted since the eighteenth century, and the well preserved original colors were copied by Colonial Williamsburg, Inc. and used extensively throughout the restoration of Williamsburg. These interior colors have been slightly modified by the current owner.

During the 1939 restoration the one and a half story frame structure now at the north end of the house was moved from the center of the land front and converted into a modern kitchen. It is supposed that this wing, said to date from 1690, was once a free-standing house located near the Perrin family graveyard a little distance from the main house. The modern south wing was added in 1954.

The fine staircase dominates the center hall. A smaller but also fine staircase ascends to the third floor. The house is also noted for its panelling, even in the bedrooms upstairs. Little England is much enhanced by the landscaping and formal gardens which form its setting.

Old frame kitchen now joined to main house

Land side

River side

Land side entrance

Panelling in second floor bedroom

Perrin family graveyard

Modern wing added 1954

Detail of door and main staircase

Smaller staircase ascends to third floor

Main staircase ascends to second floor

Little England in its garden setting

LOWLAND COTTAGE

Lowland Cottage on the Ware River was built by Robert Bristow *circa* 1670. In 1676, the plantation was raided by Bacon's rebels in search of arms, ammunition, livestock and liquor. The house has undergone many additions and alterations since Robert Bristow's 'mansion house' of two rooms up, two down on either side of a massive central chimney. The east wing was added *circa* 1785 and the back wing which now contains the kitchen *circa* 1825. Bristow's central chimney was demolished *circa* 1835. In 1854 the entire house was modernized by William Godfrey, who converted it from one and a half stories to two, and built a porch across the front. He constructed a chimney on the west end of the house. The cabin in the yard was completely reconstructed in 1963 for use as an office. Window glass was installed to take the place of the plank shutters which had served until that time.

West chimney

Artist's rendition of Lowland Cottage after 1854 alterations

90

Office, renovated 1963

Lowland Cottage on the banks of the Ware River

KEMPSVILLE

Kempsville (also known as Dragon Ordinary) was probably built in the third quarter of the eighteenth century. The loss of Gloucester County's colonial records makes it impossible to authenticate the exact date or the name of the builder. At either end of the earliest portion of the house are T-plan interior chimneys. A story and a half addition with a single dormer was added during the nineteenth century. In 1945 Kempsville was enlarged still further by the addition of a brick ell to the rear of the house. Inside the modern ell is preserved a section of the rare early clapboard roof of the main house. The south parlor contains a handsomely panelled wall. The glass-door domed cupboard to the right of the fireplace retains a fragment of mid-eighteenth century block printed floral wallpaper. The two upstairs bedrooms in the original part of the house retain their pine flooring and simple fireplaces.

1945 brick ell

Kempsville

Nineteenth century addition at right

Rare clapboard roof

Domed cupboard built into parlor panelling

Panelled parlor wall

Rare fragment of eighteenth century wallpaper

Second floor bedroom

TIMBERNECK

Timberneck stands on a high bluff overlooking Timberneck Creek and the York River, near the site of Werowicomico, the Indian Chief Powhatan's headquarters. The site is distinguished by its old trees and majestic view of the York River. The western portion of the house was built by John Catlett some time before his death in 1808. The eastern wing was added by his son, John W.C. Catlett, between 1856 and 1858. The two porches were added in this century to replace a single porch linking the two parts of the house. The wide double cross front door of the earliest section of Timberneck was brought from another older house in 1808; it retains its arrow and hatchet-proof diagonal sheathing on the inside. The original pine chimney breast survives in the northeast room. A few steps from the house stands the original gable-roofed frame smokehouse, the roof of which has a deep overhang on all four sides.

Timberneck

Detail of mid-nineteenth century east wing

Gable-roofed frame smokehouse

Two porches replace earlier large single porch

Indian-proof door

Indian-proof door

Pine chimney piece

Toddsbury

TODDSBURY

Captain Thomas Todd, ship owner, planter and member of the House of Burgesses, first came to Virginia in 1637. He took up his first land grant in Gloucester in 1651, and began work on Toddsbury on the North River between 1652 and 1660. A later addition gives the house its well-integrated L-shape. Noted architect Thomas T. Waterman saw in Toddsbury an outstanding example of those Virginia houses that are "on the edge of the stream of formal architecture…structures that are the work of master builders in which the correct detail of English handbooks is applied to purely traditional buildings. The resulting mixture," he concluded, "is a great number of excellent houses that have more native quality than formal designs, and in domestic architecture constitute a group of charm and livability." Today Toddsbury's river front bears out this description admirably in its mixture of gambrel roof and dormers with colonnade, pediment, and symmetry.

Toddsbury's colonnaded river front

L-shape is result of later addition

HESSE

In its heyday an English visitor described Hesse as "the most beautiful plantation house in Virginia." Built by leading citizen John Armistead between 1642 and 1674, the brick main house consisted of two rooms on each floor opening off the hall. The kitchen stood on the site of the present Great Room. The north wing containing the ballroom was twice as long as the rebuilt version today. The well-kept expanse of lawn sloped down to the Piankatank River in a series of terraces.

In 1797 a fire destroyed all but the present old section which fell into even greater disrepair over the next century and a half. Hesse was bought by its current owners in 1975.

Working with a skilled carpenter from nearby Gloucester, the current owners removed the nineteenth century fireplaces and restored the eighteenth century pine panelling which had been cut during the installation of the 1840's. Today it is impossible to tell where the old and new are joined. With the help of an architectural historian from Colonial Williamsburg, the same carpenter—using eighteenth century tools—designed and built new mantels as close to approximate originals as possible. A narrow closeted stairway leads to the attic where the sloping roof provides the right amount of space for a wide double canopy. Old locks and fittings were used throughout the house in the restoration.

An original sandstone cherub head survived over the seaward (east) doorway in 1975. The current owner had it copied and the copy occupies the same position on the landward side. In restoring the exterior new bricks were made in Philadelphia to match the old ones exactly. Brick by brick the chimneys were dismantled and rebuilt. To keep the materials used as authentic as possible oyster shells and sand from the river were used in the mortar.

With the aim of restoring Hesse's original symmetry, the current owners built a two-story, forty foot wing on the house's north side, and added a second floor to the matching wing on the south. Both wings follow the original foundations.

Joined to the south wing on the site of the old kitchen they have constructed a modern Great Room. One and a half stories high, lit by an enormous sunburst window, the Great Room unites the old and new elements of Hesse. A cinder block barn was turned into the pool house, with an art studio upstairs.

The current owners have overseen the landscaping and rebuilding of the shoreline terraces. The addition of tons of sand and gravel has changed an abrupt cliff into a gentle slope where a tree clings to the shore. It may yet be rescued from erosion. Further up the lawn Virginia's oldest locust grove, planted by John Armistead when he built the house, still provides summer shade.

Main staircase

Main house

Main house flanked by modern reconstruction

Restoration of eighteenth century pine panelling

Restored fireplaces

Door and staircase to third floor

Antique brass lock

Third floor bedroom

Both main entrances surmounted by sandstone cherubs

Modern Great Room

Hesse shoreline

Pool house

Oldest locust grove in Virginia

CHELSEA

Chelsea Plantation was the departure point of Governor Alexander Spotswood's "Knights of the Golden Horseshoe" expedition in 1716. The T-shaped building is formed of two distinct sections, a main block with a hipped roof erected around 1740 by Augustine Moore and a gambrel roofed addition of about 1760 probably added by Augustine's son, Bernard Moore, who married Governor Spotswood's daughter. The addition has five dormers in the southeast roof and only three in the northeast. Nineteenth century alterations included the replacing of a one-story gabled porch (the outline of which remains in the brick-work) with the two-story portico porch and a possible lowering of the roof.

The walnut entrance hall at Chelsea with its great staircase is off center like that of Westover, thus rendering the parlor to the right much larger than the other room on the first floor. This parlor is fully panelled in pine, as is the entire first floor in the 1740 section, and it has been noted that the impression of greater size in this room is enhanced by the use of arched recesses on either side of the fireplace.

Chelsea's setting is enhanced by the large formal garden of fine boxwood brought from neighboring Mount Prospect in the 1920's. Near this garden a nineteenth century schoolhouse now serves as a separate dwelling. The old kitchen survives a few steps from the house, as do the frame smokehouse and packing house.

Chelsea's unusual T-shape

Circa 1740 main block

Chelsea

Walnut entrance hall

Drawing room arches

Kitchen

Two views of 1760 addition

Nineteenth century schoolhouse stands in formal garden

Smokehouse and packing house

105

ELSING GREEN

Elsing Green, one of the most imposing of the Virginia mansions, was built in 1758 by Carter Braxton, a wealthy planter. This date is attested to by an inscribed brick, now hidden, over the west door.

While the wide river front of Elsing Green alone is enough to grant it distinction, it is the mansion's unique U-shaped plan and the resulting court which give such an impression of immense size. The feeling of immensity is augmented by its location on a series of high terraces overlooking the Pamunkey River. The east and west entrances are also exceedingly grand by Virginia standards.

Everywhere Elsing Green is a symphony in symmetry. This begins with the wings, each containing a single room. The narrow windows and square chimney stacks here resemble those in the end elevations of Chelsea. It has been noted that the size and formality of the plantation complex at Elsing Green is greatly enhanced by the placement of the dependencies. The story and a half principal dependencies parallel the long axis of the mansion. The eastern, and older dependency, is believed to date from between 1690 and 1719. The western, a restored kitchen, dates from the nineteenth century. Inside, the symmetry is maintained by a staircase and an immense cooking fireplace at either end. A brick smokehouse and dairy are aligned vertically with the kitchen and other principal dependency to form a forecourt facing the river; the formal effect is heightened by two further small square brick dependencies two terraces down aligned with the smokehouse and dairy.

The hall-passage plan of the main house is noteworthy. A short hall opening from the river front is set slightly off center, like the central hall at Westover and Chelsea, to allow for a parlor larger than its corresponding room across the hall. This hall opens into a cross hall, running the width of the house, which contains a staircase at each end. The double stairs descend to the basement and ascend to the third floor, thus reinforcing the theme of symmetry.

High terraces add to Elsing Green's impression of great size

Mansion flanked by two principal dependencies

U-shaped land front

106

River front

Wings blanace each other in perfect symmetry

East entrance

107

Western dependency contains a restored kitchen

Kitchen fireplace

Detail of terraces and dependencies

PLEASANT GREEN

Pleasant Green, an eighteenth century brick house, was built by a member of the Timberlake family. According to tradition the construction took place after the winning of a London lottery.

Pleasant Green follows the central hall and two room plan. From the outside both sides of the main block are identical. Restored, it is now the main house on a thousand acre farm.

Pleasant Green

SWEET HALL

Sweet Hall stands on a lovely site overlooking a wide bend in the Pamunkey River. The house, believed to have been built by Captain Thomas Claiborne around 1725, is remarkable for the number of rare architectural features it contains.

Sweet Hall is an off-center L-shaped house. The main block consists of a hall and chamber with an original attached kitchen forming the ell to the rear. The further small frame attachment is twentieth century; the porches are nineteenth. The house's medieval air shows the persistence of seventeenth century and earlier building practices into the early eighteenth. These details include the elaborate T-shaped stacks of the main block's interior end chimneys. The sharp pitch of the roof, the resultant impressive gables, and the huge steep pyramid chimney are medieval features which occasionally persisted into the eighteenth century in Virginia. Most notable of all is the upper cruck construction of the roof, the only roof of this type known in Virginia and one of three in America. A remarkable holdover of medieval building practices, the upper cruck is a curved timber set on top of a tie beam built between the walls, rising up to the apex of the roof and forming the upper story. At Sweet Hall, the upper crucks are found in the gable ends and are particularly noticeable in the east bedroom.

Original attached kitchen gives Sweet Hall an L-shape

Sweet Hall

Sweet Hall

Upper cruck visible in second floor bedroom

T-shaped chimney stacks

Pyramid chimney

WYOMING

According to tradition Wyoming was built between 1791 and 1800. This farmhouse, which occupies an imposing position on a hill overlooking the Pamunkey River flats, is large for the area, which was not opened for settlement until 1700 when the Indians were finally subdued. Most eighteenth century houses here tend to be small homesteads.

Wyoming is remarkable for its combination of size and simplicity with a few elaborate touches of ornamentation. On either side of the house a modillioned cornice runs the length of the roof. The brickwork of the exterior end chimneys is of Flemish bond. The roof has clipped gables. The first floor plan consists of a center hall flanked by a single large room on either side; the twenty-five foot depth of the house makes each of these rooms very large indeed. The parlor to the left of the entrance door contains the magnificent pine chimney breast. The room is also fully wainscoted, as is the rest of the first floor. The current owner relates that Colonial Williamsburg had approached his mother with an offer to buy the panelling and wainscoting but her reply had been, "Absolutely not. What would my house look like without it?" The staircase is completely enclosed and a narrow cord serves as a banister.

Wyoming

Flemish bond brickwork

Clipped-end gables

112

Cornice at roof line

Stately pine chimney breast

Enclosed staircase

113

WOODLAWN

With its picturesque "catslide" roof Woodlawn presents a different face to the world from whatever direction it is viewed. The house was built in the mid-eighteenth century by the Haile family, and the current owner believes it to be the last original saltbox house in Essex County. During restoration work the owner found the basement rafters to be continuous throughout the house, proof that the entire house was built at one time. These heavy beams run from the kitchen at the rear through the basement dining room, where stairs were added in the 1860's when the Trible family took up residence. Before their arrival, all ascent and descent between floors had been by ladder; stairs leading from the first to the second floor were also added at this time.

Woodlawn's restoration was carried out almost singlehandledly by the current owner, who had fallen in love with the house and bought it to save it from being bulldozed into the ground. The product of her efforts is remarkably the same as the house in 1910. Throughout the house she has been scrupulous in her preservation of period detail. The house retained its original doors which have five raised panels; a single panel at the top replaces the usual two square panels of a six-panel door. Most of these doors still have their original wooden string latches, such as in the first floor rear room and upstairs bedroom. The window trim is original, as is much of the window glass. Wherever possible the owner tried to reproduce the colors used in the first painting of the house. She also used suitable materials from other old houses such as the leather washers and hinges on a hall door.

Woodlawn, three views

Kitchen

Stairs a nineteenth century addition

Woodlawn, 1910

Wooden string latch, first floor

Original five-panel door

Wooden string latch, second floor bedroom

Living room view of original window trim and glass

FOX HILL PLANTATION

Fox Hill, flounder house lean-to at right

1761 south block, originally main entrance

Fox Hill is an L-shaped house which the current owner believes was built in three distinct stages. The first, a small lean-to structure containing the modern kitchen, was built as a "flounder house," a house built to secure a property grant. The south block was added to the lean-to in 1761. The date is inscribed on a windowsill in the cellar. Richard Selden acquired the plantation in 1793 and added the north block containing another staircase hall and one room on each floor in 1803. The resulting east front, the main entrance today, is scarcely distinguishable at first glance from the typical eighteenth century rectangular central hall-two room house.

Two original outbuildings survive. The two-story old kitchen is directly south of the main house and aligned with it in the manner of a flanking dependency. It boasts fine Flemish bond brickwork and the current owner believes that it may have been lived in by the Fox family, the first owners of the plantation, while the larger house was being built, and that later it may have served as a dower house as well as a plantation kitchen. West of the kitchen stands an original brick smokehouse.

The completed L-shaped house has two large stair halls, that in the later addition being slightly more elaborate than the one of 1761. It is now the principal entry. The north parlor is the most ornate, although throughout the house the woodwork is elegant yet restrained and there are no striking discrepancies between the additions. A pair of rounded-arch niches flanking the fireplace adds to the feeling of spaciousness. Here and throughout the first floor the trim is painted in "Fox Hill Green" a color mixed by the current owner especially for the house. The southeast parlor, now the library, is similar in design, with the niches now serving as cupboards. It has been noted that the brickwork of the original jack arch over the fireplace, which was never plastered, is of high quality. The dining room located in the rear ell was originally a bedchamber. Its mantel is less adorned than the other two.

The original owner, David Fox, had called this the Hill Plantation. Richard Selden apparently renamed it Farmville, and this was the name under which the current owner acquired it during the 1940's. She renamed it Fox Hill in honor of the original owner. Larger in manner than in actual size, Fox Hill represents an old Virginia plantation house not too large to be comfortably liveable in the twentieth century.

Kitchen

1803 north block addition and old kitchen

117

Smokehouse

Detail of 1803 staircase

1803 staircase, now principal entry

North parlor

Dining room

Library

SABINE HALL

Sabine Hall was built in 1730 for Landon Carter, a younger son of Robert "King" Carter, in his day the largest landowner in Virginia. The original house was a square block (Sheets 48 & 49) flanked by separate brick dependencies. During alterations in the 1840's the roof was lowered, the north portico added, and the low porch across the south front constructed on the site of an old paved terrace.

The house is of the center-hall plan (Sheets 50, 51, 52). Although the door and transom (Sheet 53) are not original, they are in keeping with the rest of the house. The interior woodwork is especially worthy of note, being virtually unchanged since it was installed (Sheets 54, 55, 56, 57, 58). The two wide arches at either end of the sweeping staircase are especially grand (Sheets 59 & 60), as is the staircase itself (Sheet 61). The second floor hall boasts original interior shutters. There is also an interesting stone mantel in the study whose origin is unknown. The paint color for this and the other rooms was mixed to the specifications of the current owner, a direct descendant of Landon Carter.

A series of sloping terraces separates Sabine Hall from the Rappahannock River. On the river side of the house is a formal garden modelled on Landon Carter's original, some of which survives in an ancient boxwood walk to the southeast of the house (Sheet 62). The picturesque old barn lies not far from the house.

For additional architectural drawings see sheets 63, 64, 65).

Sabine Hall entrance

Sabine Hall

119

North portico added 1840's

South front

First floor staircase arch

Second floor staircase arch

Original interior shutters

Old barn

Stone mantel surmounted by portrait of Landon Carter, the builder

TUCKAHOE

There are many theories regarding Tuckahoe's construction, one of which is that Tuckahoe began as a single wooden rectangular house built on the central hall-two room plan by Thomas Randolph some time around 1712. This earlier portion of the house forms the southern block and river front of the now H-shaped dwelling. It appears that when Thomas's son William married in 1735 and needed more space he differed from his wealthy planter contemporaries in deciding not to demolish the wooden house he had inherited. Choosing a more economical path, he added on to it, making a virtue of necessity by constructing the house in its final unusual form. There were precedents in the colony for this form in the Lees' great brick house Stratford Hall and in the Williamsburg Capitol of 1699, and William Randolph may have had them in mind when he conceived the overall plan of his addition. By giving it a T-shape rather than merely adding on a rectangle, as at Chelsea, he created a house which is uniquely satisfying in many ways.

Tuckahoe is unusual in having no clearly defined front or back. Due to its H-shape it presents a distinct whole to any of the four points of the compass. The courtyard where the 1712 house to the right joins with the later construction stands on its own as an example of the symmetrical design so beloved by eighteenth century Virginians. The mixture of brick with frame makes the courtyard effect at Tuckahoe less formal than that of Elsing Green.

Tuckahoe's two end units, as well as the connecting one are but one room in depth. The current owners find that they live more in the older south wing, which contains the modern kitchen in the basement. The stair hall here is simple but formal in design. The panelling is pine, as it is throughout this wing and in the cross hall directly beyond. The south door is the most ornate in the house and appears to be an amalgamation of two plates of William Salmon's *Palladio Londoniensis*. The north stair hall is walnut. Its highly ornate stair brackets contrast forcibly with the simpler design of those in the southern wing. A carved basket of flowers design decorates the landing. The two rooms on the first floor are also fully panelled in walnut. That on the east is known as the 'Burnt Room' as it was singed by fire in the eighteenth century. The mantel is probably early nineteenth century.

Tuckahoe is renowned for its "street" of plantation outbuildings. Their survival has allowed Tuckahoe to retain the village-like aspect which so charmed early English visitors. Not far from the house stand the old kitchen, barn, office and smokehouse. The north and west cabins have served as bachelor quarters for visitors or housing for the cook and butler. Today a resident handyman lives in one; another is rented. To the west of the house, away from the "street" stands the little schoolhouse where Thomas Jefferson had lessons with his Randolph cousins when he lived at Tuckahoe from 1745 to 1752.

North front

122

Tuckahoe, river front

East front

Courtyard effect

Pine south stair hall

South door

124   *Walnut north stair hall*

Stair bracket, north hall

Stair bracket, south hall

Basket of flowers

Plantation street

Burnt room

Main house and dependencies

Cabin

Thomas Jefferson's schoolhouse

Photography Credits

I am indebted to the Virginia Historic Landmark Commission and the Virginia State Library for the use of the black and white photographs of Wolftrap Farm, Poplar Springs, The Rowe (top photo only on page 65), Criss Cross, Lowland Cottage, Timberneck, Chelsea, Sweet Hall, and Wyoming. The black and white photographs of the Allmand-Archer House are from the collection of the current owner, and the color on page 18 (top row center, and bottom) and 19 (top row left and right, bottom row right) are by Nelson A. Danish. The black and white photographs in the lower right hand corner of page 23 and that on the top of page 24 are from the collection of the current owner of the Selden House. The current owner of Hesse supplied the color photographs on the top row of page 100. The black and white photograph of Woodlawn is from the collection of the current owner.

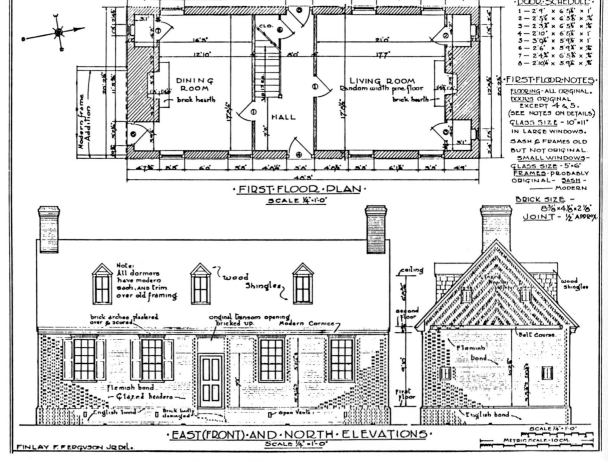

(Sheet 1)

Adam Keeling House

(Sheet 2)

Adam Keeling House

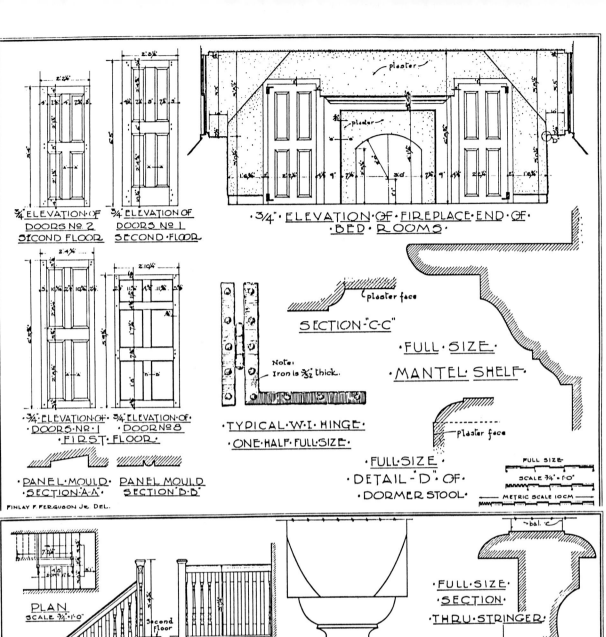

(Sheet 3)

Adam Keeling House

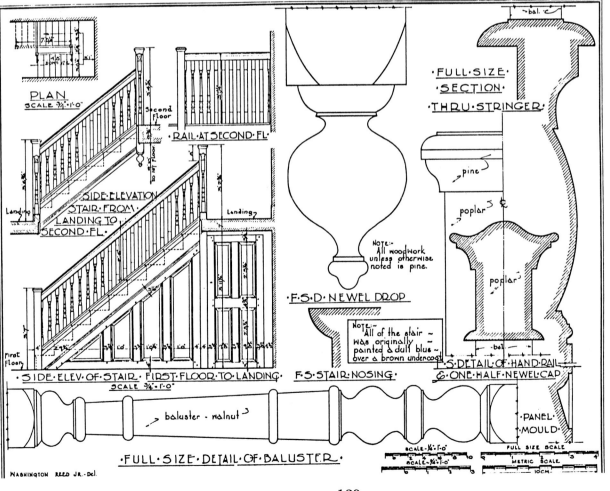

(Sheet 4)

Adam Keeling House

129

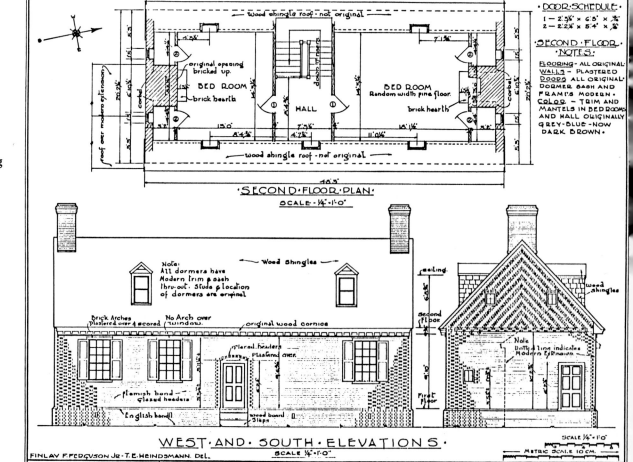

SECTION
THRU
PILASTER FLUTE

PANELLED·NORTH·END·LIVING·ROOM·
SCALE·¾"·1'·0"

PILASTER
BASE

PANEL MOULD

CHAIR RAIL

PEDESTAL
BASE

FULL SIZE

TYPICAL
DOOR TRIM
Typical trim
as dotted.

MANTEL SHELF

FULL·SIZE·CORNICE

BASE

NASHINGTON REED JR. Del.

·SECOND·FLOOR·PLAN·
SCALE·¼"·1'·0"

·DOOR·SCHEDULE·

·SECOND·FLOOR·
NOTES·

WEST·AND·SOUTH·ELEVATIONS·
SCALE·¼"·1'·0"

FINLAY F. FERGUSON JR · T. E. HEINDSMANN. DEL.

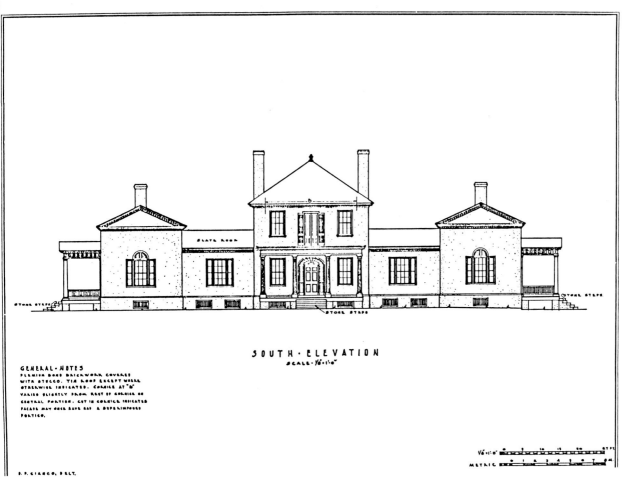

SOUTH·ELEVATION
SCALE ⅛"·1'-0"

GENERAL·NOTES

PRESENT BODY BRICKWORK COVERED
WITH STUCCO. TILE ROOF EXCEPT WHERE
OTHERWISE INDICATED. CORNICE AT "b"
VARIES SLIGHTLY FROM REST OF CORNICE OR
CENTRAL PORTION. CUT IN CORNICE INDICATED
FACADE MAY ONCE HAVE HAD A SUPERIMPOSED
PORTICO.

D.P. CIANCO, DELT.

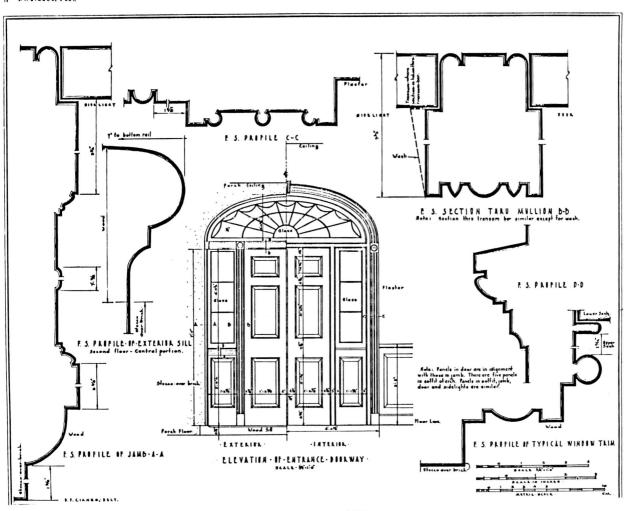

F.S. PROFILE C-C

F.S. SECTION THRU MULLION B-B
Note: Section thru transom bar similar except for wash.

F.S. PROFILE D-D

F.S. PROFILE OF EXTERIOR SILL
Second floor - Central portion.

Note: Panels in door are in alignment
with those in jamb. There are five panels
in soffit of arch. Panels in soffit, jamb,
door and sidelights are similar.

F.S. PROFILE OF JAMB-A-A

ELEVATION·OF·ENTRANCE·DOORWAY·
SCALE ¾"·1'-0"

F.S. PROFILE OF TYPICAL WINDOW TRIM

D.P. CIANCO, DELT.

131

(Sheet 9)

Battersea

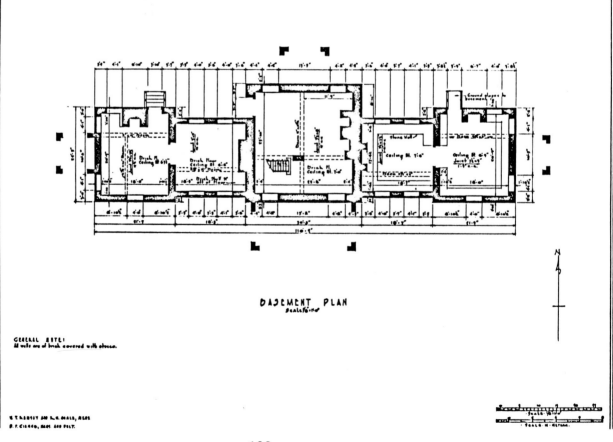

WEST ELEVATION OF STAIR HALL

SECTION THRU STAIRHALL SHOWING STAIRWAY

(Sheet 10)

Battersea

BASEMENT PLAN

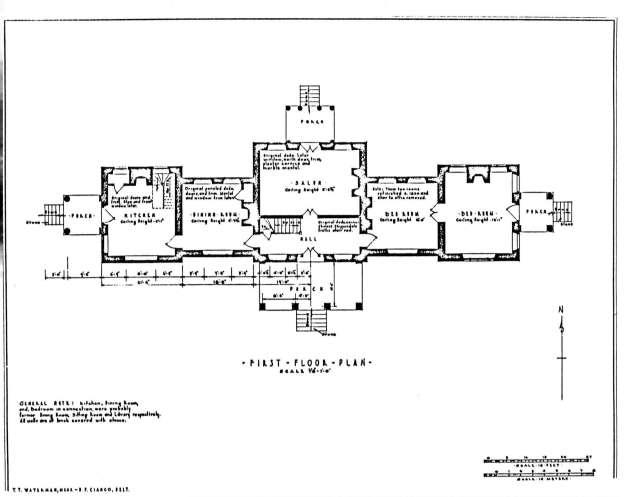

(Sheet 11)

Battersea

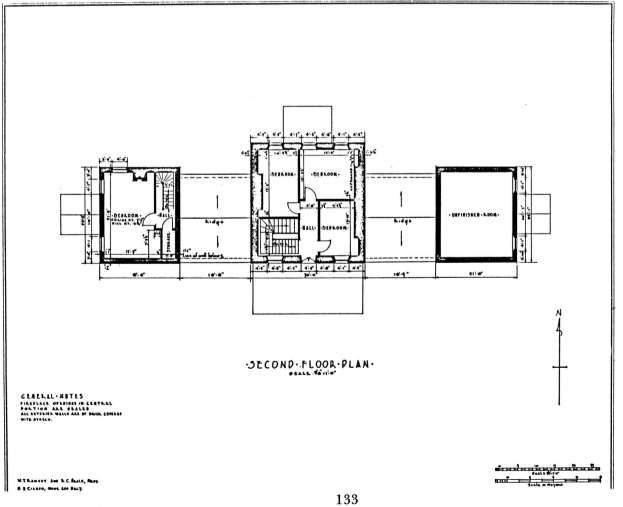

(Sheet 12)

Battersea

133

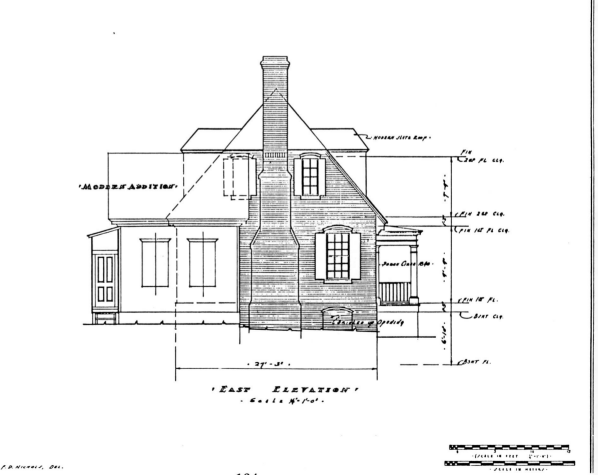

(Sheet 13)

Sheild
House

'WEST ELEVATION'
Scale ¼"=1'-0"

F. D. NICHOLS, DEL.

(Sheet 14)

Sheild
House

'EAST ELEVATION'
Scale ¼"=1'-0"

F. D. NICHOLS, DEL.

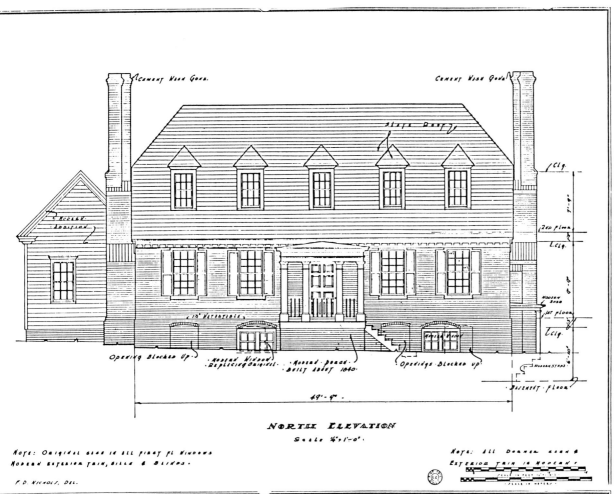

(Sheet 15)

Sheild House

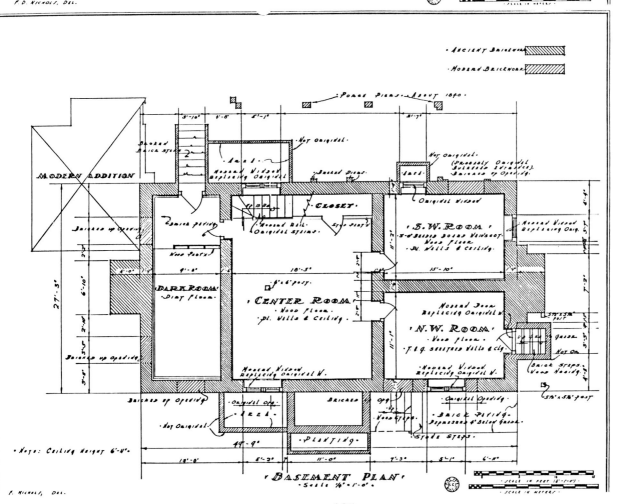

(Sheet 16)

Sheild House

(Sheet 17)

Sheild
House

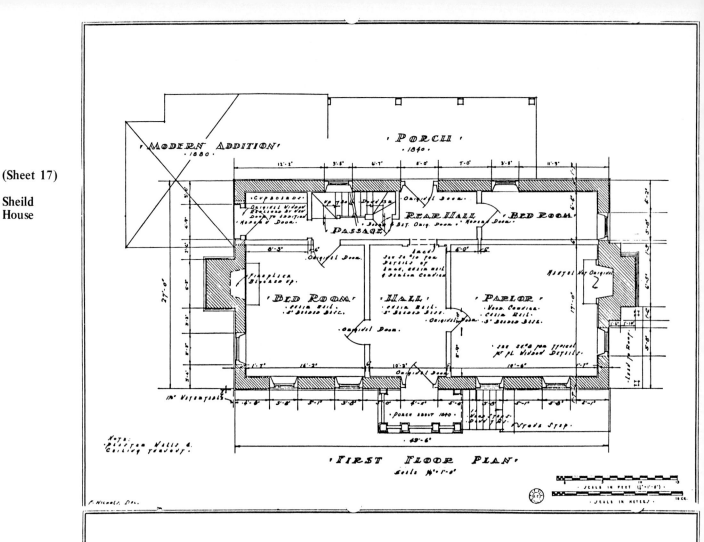

(Sheet 18)

Sheild
House

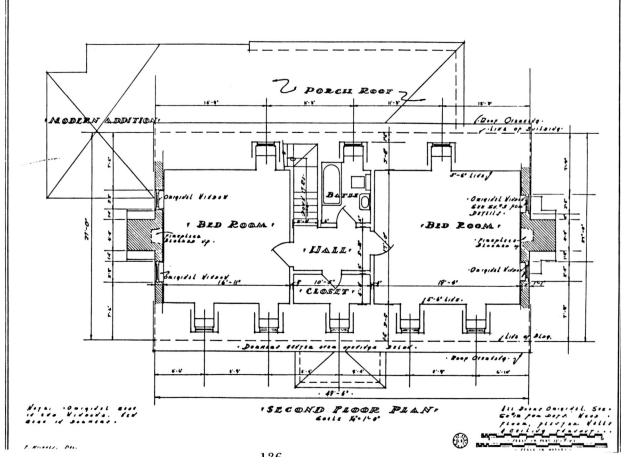

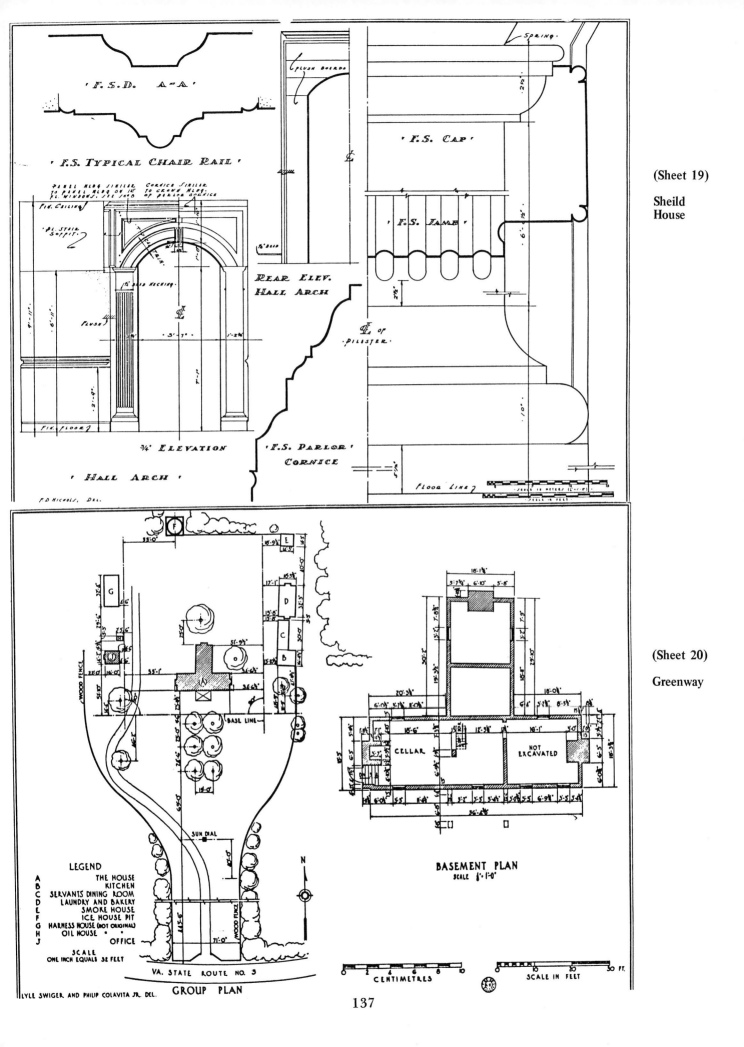

'F.S.D. A-A'

'F.S. TYPICAL CHAIR RAIL'

'F.S. CAP'

'F.S. JAMB'

REAR ELEV.
HALL ARCH

¾' ELEVATION

'F.S. PARLOR'
CORNICE

'HALL ARCH'

F.D.NICHOLS, DEL.

(Sheet 19)

Sheild
House

(Sheet 20)

Greenway

BASEMENT PLAN
SCALE ¼'·1'-0'

LEGEND
A   THE HOUSE
B   KITCHEN
C   SERVANTS DINING ROOM
D   LAUNDRY AND BAKERY
E   SMOKE HOUSE
F   ICE HOUSE PIT
G   HARNESS HOUSE (NOT ORIGINAL)
H   OIL HOUSE
J   OFFICE

SCALE
ONE INCH EQUALS 32 FEET

CELLAR

NOT
EXCAVATED

SUN DIAL

N

CENTIMETRES

SCALE IN FEET

VA. STATE ROUTE NO. 5

GROUP PLAN

LYLE SWIGER AND PHILIP COLAVITA JR. DEL.

137

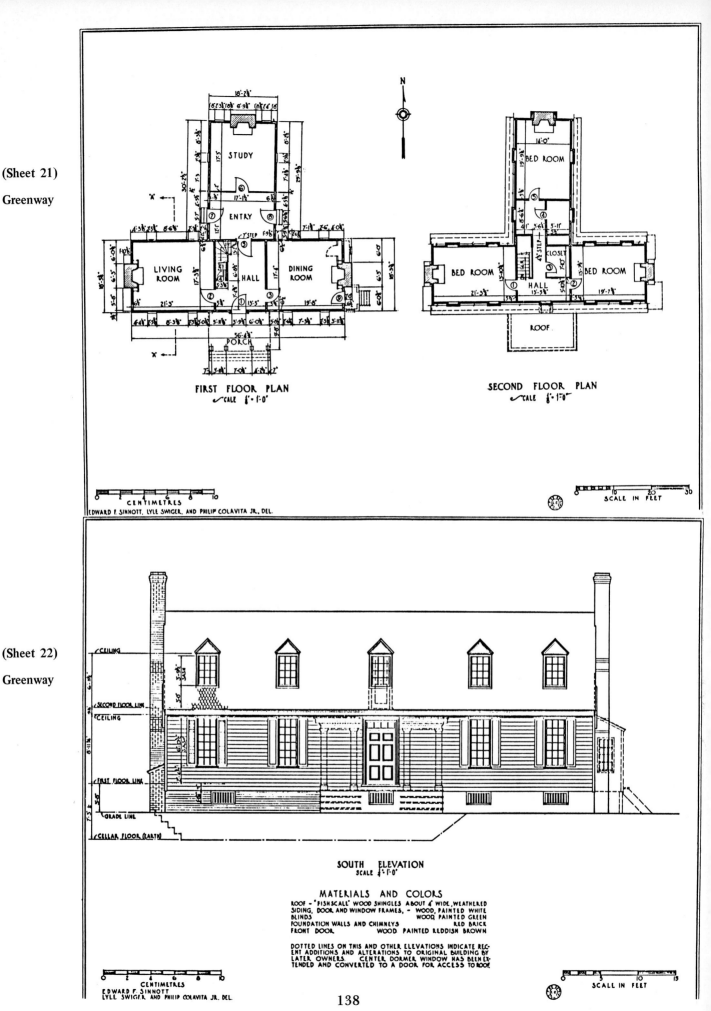

STUDY

ENTRY

LIVING
ROOM

HALL

DINING
ROOM

PORCH

FIRST FLOOR PLAN
SCALE ⅛"=1'-0"

BED ROOM

BED ROOM

HALL

CLOSET

BED ROOM

ROOF

SECOND FLOOR PLAN
SCALE ⅛"=1'-0"

CENTIMETRES

EDWARD F. SINNOTT, LYLE SWIGER, AND PHILIP COLAVITA JR. DEL.

SCALE IN FEET

CEILING

SECOND FLOOR LINE
CEILING

FIRST FLOOR LINE

GRADE LINE

CELLAR FLOOR (EARTH)

SOUTH ELEVATION
SCALE ¼"=1'-0"

MATERIALS AND COLORS

ROOF - "FISH SCALE" WOOD SHINGLES ABOUT 4" WIDE, WEATHERED
SIDING, DOOR AND WINDOW FRAMES, - WOOD, PAINTED WHITE
BLINDS   WOOD PAINTED GREEN
FOUNDATION WALLS AND CHIMNEYS   RED BRICK
FRONT DOOR   WOOD PAINTED REDDISH BROWN

DOTTED LINES ON THIS AND OTHER ELEVATIONS INDICATE REC-
ENT ADDITIONS AND ALTERATIONS TO ORIGINAL BUILDING BY
LATER OWNERS.   CENTER DORMER WINDOW HAS BEEN EX-
TENDED AND CONVERTED TO A DOOR FOR ACCESS TO ROOF.

CENTIMETRES

EDWARD F. SINNOTT
LYLE SWIGER AND PHILIP COLAVITA JR. DEL.

SCALE IN FEET

138

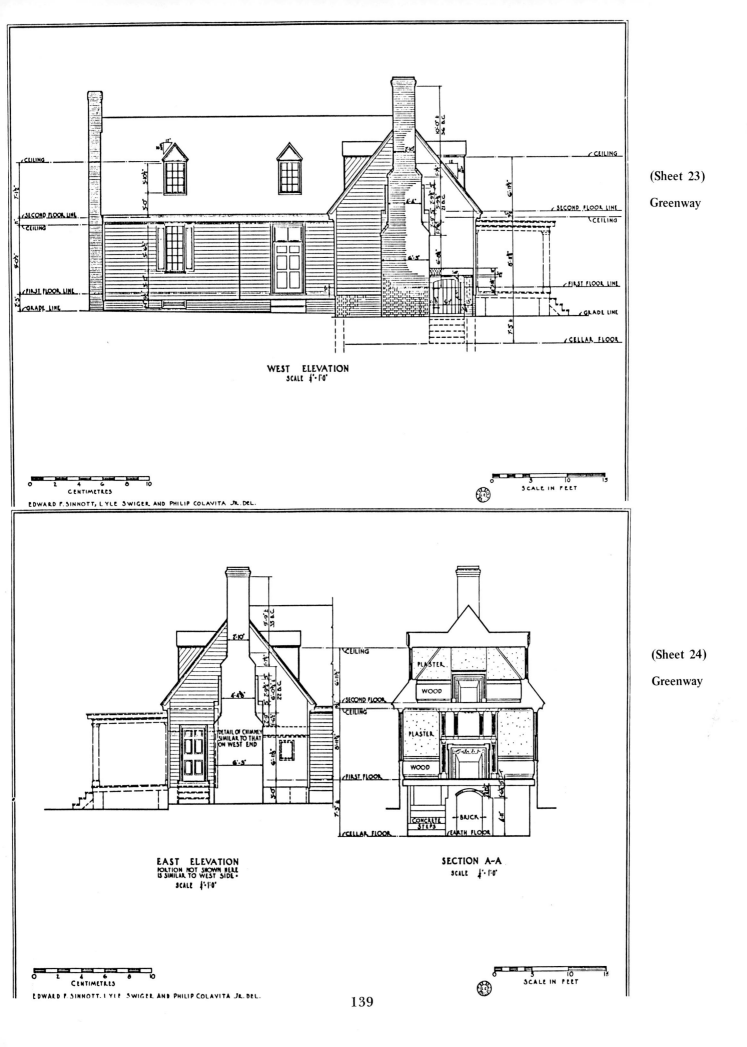

WEST ELEVATION
SCALE ¼"=1'0"

EDWARD F. SINNOTT, LYLE SWIGER AND PHILIP COLAVITA JR. DEL.

CENTIMETRES
0 2 4 6 8 10

SCALE IN FEET
0   5   10   15

(Sheet 23)
Greenway

EAST ELEVATION
PORTION NOT SHOWN HERE
IS SIMILAR TO WEST SIDE·
SCALE ¼"=1'0"

SECTION A-A
SCALE ¼"=1'0"

DETAIL OF CHIMNEY
SIMILAR TO THAT
ON WEST END

PLASTER

WOOD

PLASTER

WOOD

CONCRETE
STEPS

BRICK

EARTH FLOOR

(Sheet 24)
Greenway

EDWARD F. SINNOTT, LYLE SWIGER AND PHILIP COLAVITA JR. DEL.

CENTIMETRES
0 2 4 6 8 10

SCALE IN FEET
0   5   10   15

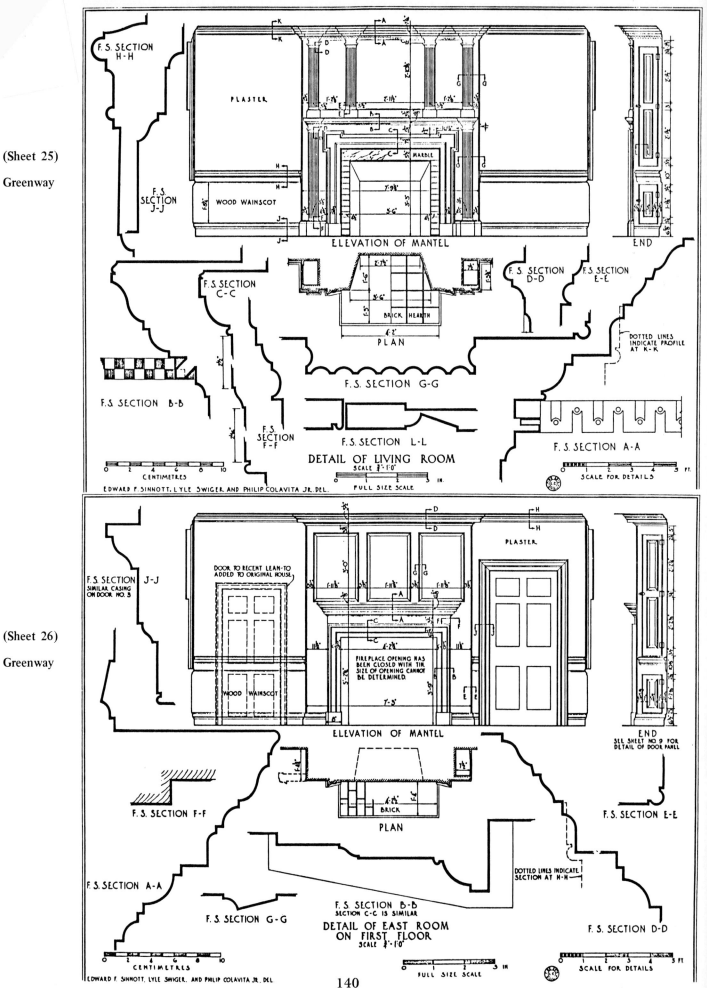

(Sheet 25)

Greenway

F.S. SECTION
H-H

PLASTER

F.S.
SECTION
J-J

WOOD WAINSCOT

ELEVATION OF MANTEL

MARBLE

7'-9½'

5'-6'

END

F.S. SECTION
C-C

F.S. SECTION B-B

F.S.
SECTION
F-F

2'-7½'

5'-6'

BRICK HEARTH

4'-2'

PLAN

F. S. SECTION
D-D

F.S. SECTION
E-E

DOTTED LINES
INDICATE PROFILE
AT K-K

F.S. SECTION G-G

F.S. SECTION L-L

DETAIL OF LIVING ROOM

SCALE ¾'-1'0'

F.S. SECTION A-A

CENTIMETRES

FULL SIZE SCALE

SCALE FOR DETAILS

EDWARD F. SINNOTT, LYLE SWIGER AND PHILIP COLAVITA JR. DEL.

(Sheet 26)

Greenway

F.S. SECTION J-J
SIMILAR CASING
ON DOOR NO. 5

DOOR TO RECENT LEAN-TO
ADDED TO ORIGINAL HOUSE

5'-0'

FIREPLACE OPENING HAS
BEEN CLOSED WITH TIN.
SIZE OF OPENING CANNOT
BE DETERMINED.

7'-5'

WOOD WAINSCOT

ELEVATION OF MANTEL

PLASTER

END
SEE SHEET NO. 9 FOR
DETAIL OF DOOR PANEL

F. S. SECTION F-F

4'-2½'

BRICK

PLAN

F.S. SECTION E-E

F. S. SECTION A-A

F. S. SECTION G-G

F. S. SECTION B-B
SECTION C-C IS SIMILAR

DOTTED LINES INDICATE
SECTION AT H-H

DETAIL OF EAST ROOM
ON FIRST FLOOR

SCALE ¾'-1'0'

F. S. SECTION D-D

CENTIMETRES

FULL SIZE SCALE

SCALE FOR DETAILS

EDWARD F. SINNOTT, LYLE SWIGER, AND PHILIP COLAVITA JR. DEL.

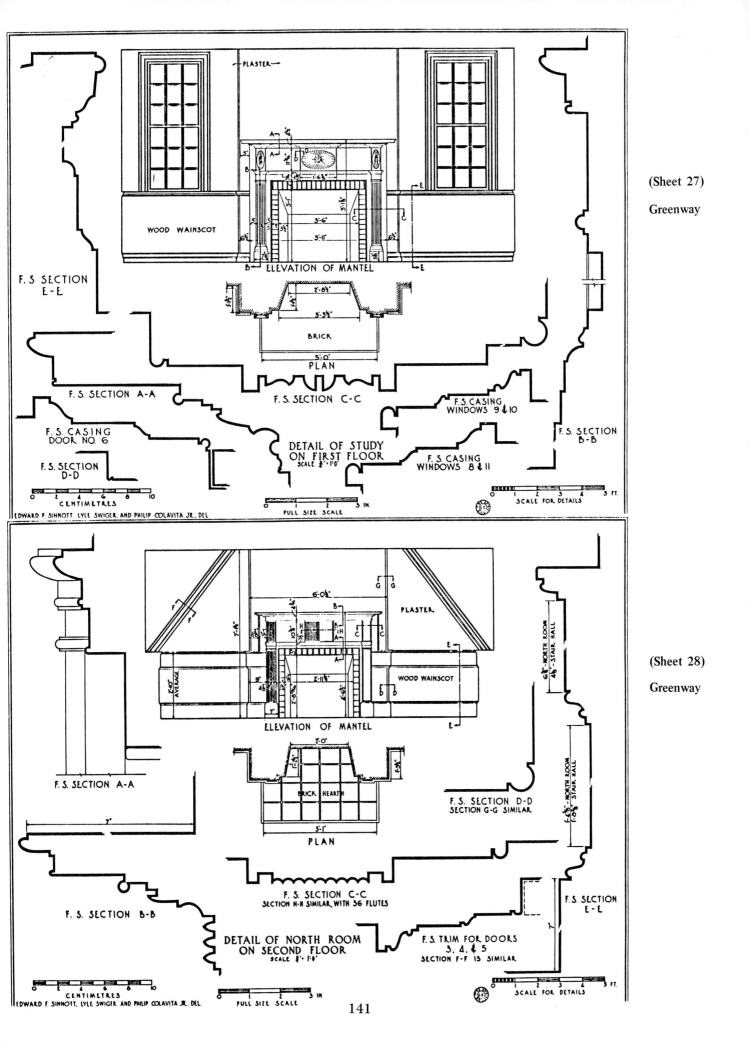

(Sheet 27)

Greenway

PLASTER

WOOD WAINSCOT

ELEVATION OF MANTEL

F. S SECTION
E - E

BRICK

PLAN

F.S SECTION A-A

F.S. SECTION C-C

F.S. CASING
WINDOWS 9 & 10

F.S CASING
DOOR NO. 6

F.S SECTION
B-B

F. S. SECTION
D-D

DETAIL OF STUDY
ON FIRST FLOOR
SCALE ¾" = 1'0"

F.S. CASING
WINDOWS 8 & 11

0 2 4 6 8 10
CENTIMETRES

0   1   2   3 IN.
FULL SIZE SCALE

0 1 2 3 4 5 FT.
SCALE FOR DETAILS

EDWARD F. SINNOTT, LYLE SWIGER, AND PHILIP COLAVITA JR., DEL.

(Sheet 28)

Greenway

PLASTER

WOOD WAINSCOT

ELEVATION OF MANTEL

F.S. SECTION A-A

BRICK HEARTH

PLAN

F. S. SECTION D-D
SECTION G-G SIMILAR

F.S. SECTION
E - E

F.S. SECTION B-B

F. S. SECTION C-C
SECTION H-H SIMILAR, WITH 36 FLUTES

DETAIL OF NORTH ROOM
ON SECOND FLOOR
SCALE ¾" = 1'0"

F. S. TRIM FOR DOORS
3, 4, & 5
SECTION F-F IS SIMILAR

0 2 4 6 8 10
CENTIMETRES

0   1   2   3 IN.
FULL SIZE SCALE

0 1 2 3 4 5 FT.
SCALE FOR DETAILS

EDWARD F. SINNOTT, LYLE SWIGER AND PHILIP COLAVITA JR., DEL.

141

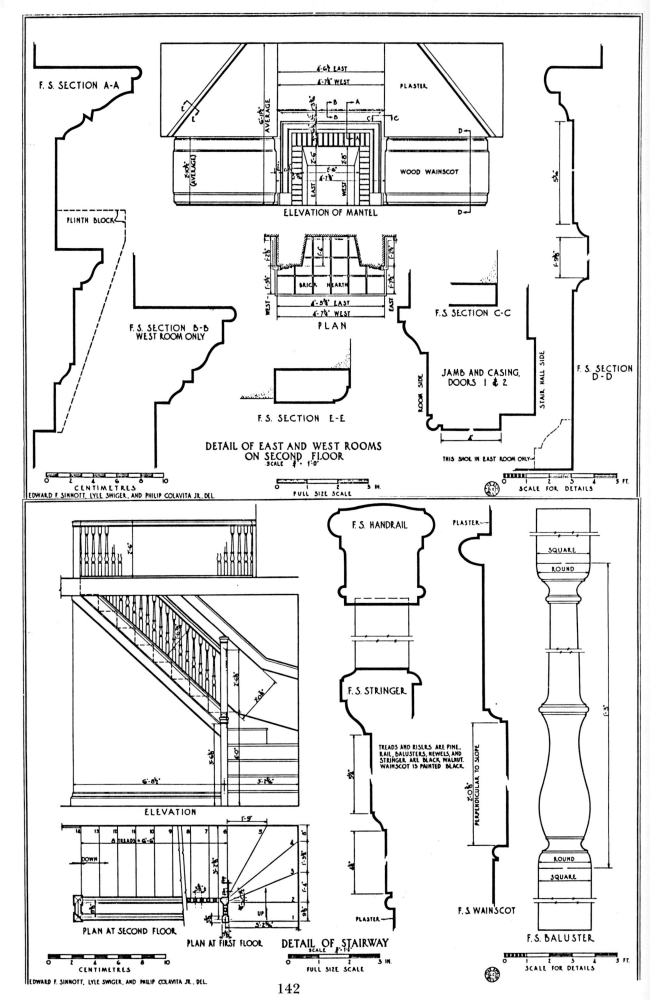

F. S. SECTION A-A

4'-6½" EAST
4'-7⅞" WEST

PLASTER

PLINTH BLOCK

6'-1½" AVERAGE

2'-0½" (AVERAGE)

ELEVATION OF MANTEL

WOOD WAINSCOT

F. S. SECTION B-B
WEST ROOM ONLY

BRICK HEARTH

4'-5⅝" EAST
4'-7½" WEST

WEST 1'-5½"

EAST 1'-7½"

P L A N

F.S. SECTION C-C

F.S. SECTION E-E

ROOM SIDE

JAMB AND CASING,
DOORS 1 & 2

STAIR HALL SIDE

F. S. SECTION
D-D

DETAIL OF EAST AND WEST ROOMS
ON SECOND FLOOR
SCALE ¾" = 1'0"

THIS SHOE IN EAST ROOM ONLY

0 2 4 6 8 10
CENTIMETRES
EDWARD F. SINNOTT, LYLE SWIGER, AND PHILIP COLAVITA JR. DEL.

0   1   2   3 IN.
FULL SIZE SCALE

0 1 2 3 4 5 FT.
SCALE FOR DETAILS

F. S. HANDRAIL

PLASTER

SQUARE

ROUND

ELEVATION

F. S. STRINGER

6'-0½"

2'-6"

3'-8¼"

5'-6"

5'-0"

3'-2¾"

PLAN AT SECOND FLOOR

8 TREADS = 6'-6"

DOWN

UP

PLAN AT FIRST FLOOR

TREADS AND RISERS ARE PINE.
RAIL, BALUSTERS, NEWELS, AND
STRINGER ARE BLACK WALNUT.
WAINSCOT IS PAINTED BLACK.

PERPENDICULAR TO SLOPE

F.S. WAINSCOT

PLASTER

ROUND

SQUARE

DETAIL OF STAIRWAY
SCALE ¾" = 1'-0"

1'-9"

1'-9½"

1'-9"

0 2 4 6 8 10
CENTIMETRES

0   1   2   3 IN.
FULL SIZE SCALE

0 1 2 3 4 5 FT.
SCALE FOR DETAILS

F.S. BALUSTER

EDWARD F. SINNOTT, LYLE SWIGER, AND PHILIP COLAVITA JR. DEL.

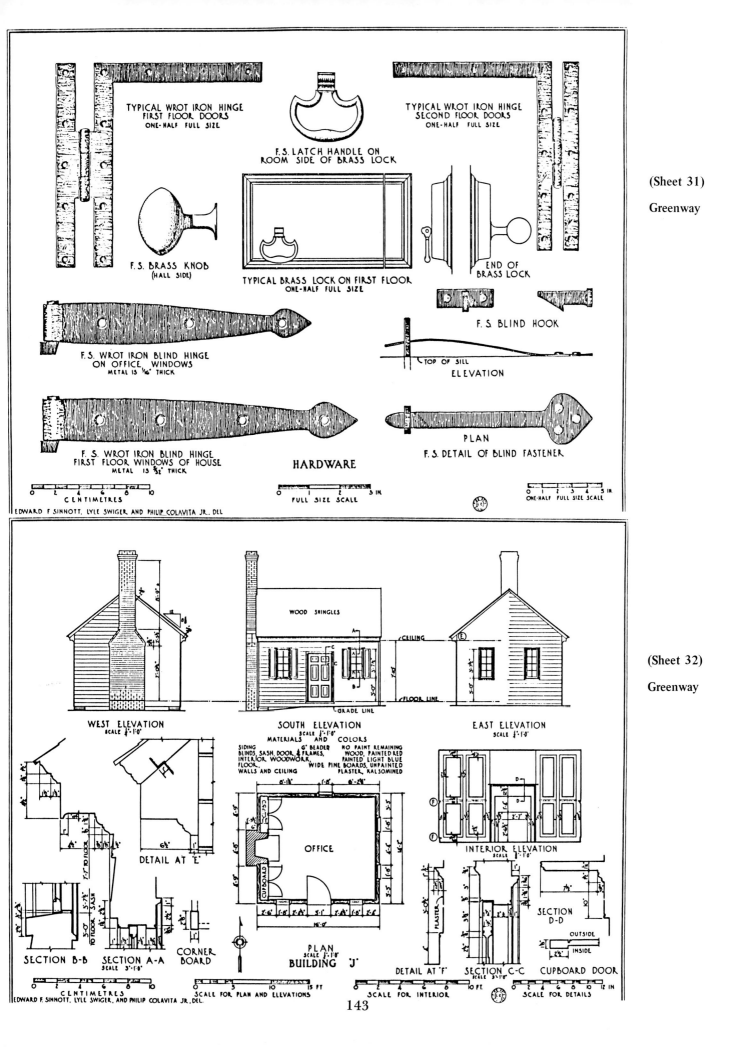

TYPICAL WROT IRON HINGE
FIRST FLOOR DOORS
ONE-HALF FULL SIZE

F.S. LATCH HANDLE ON
ROOM SIDE OF BRASS LOCK

TYPICAL WROT IRON HINGE
SECOND FLOOR DOORS
ONE-HALF FULL SIZE

F.S. BRASS KNOB
(HALL SIDE)

TYPICAL BRASS LOCK ON FIRST FLOOR
ONE-HALF FULL SIZE

END OF
BRASS LOCK

F.S. WROT IRON BLIND HINGE
ON OFFICE WINDOWS
METAL IS 1/16" THICK

F.S. BLIND HOOK

TOP OF SILL
ELEVATION

F.S. WROT IRON BLIND HINGE
FIRST FLOOR WINDOWS OF HOUSE
METAL IS 3/32" THICK

HARDWARE

PLAN

F.S. DETAIL OF BLIND FASTENER

CENTIMETRES

FULL SIZE SCALE

ONE-HALF FULL SIZE SCALE

EDWARD F. SINNOTT, LYLE SWIGER AND PHILIP COLAVITA JR., DEL.

(Sheet 31)

Greenway

WOOD SHINGLES

CEILING

FLOOR LINE

GRADE LINE

WEST ELEVATION
SCALE 1/4"=1'-0"

SOUTH ELEVATION
SCALE 1/4"=1'-0"

EAST ELEVATION
SCALE 1/4"=1'-0"

MATERIALS AND COLORS

SIDING   6" BEADER   NO PAINT REMAINING
BLINDS, SASH, DOOR, & FRAMES,   WOOD, PAINTED RED
INTERIOR WOODWORK,   PAINTED LIGHT BLUE
FLOOR,   WIDE PINE BOARDS, UNPAINTED
WALLS AND CEILING   PLASTER, KALSOMINED

DETAIL AT 'E'

INTERIOR ELEVATION
SCALE 1/2"=1'-0"

OFFICE

CUPBOARD

SECTION B-B

SECTION A-A
SCALE 3"=1'-0"

CORNER
BOARD

PLAN
SCALE 1/4"=1'-0"
BUILDING 'J'

DETAIL AT 'F'

SECTION C-C
SCALE 3"=1'-0"

SECTION D-D

OUTSIDE
INSIDE

CUPBOARD DOOR

CENTIMETRES

SCALE FOR PLAN AND ELEVATIONS

SCALE FOR INTERIOR

SCALE FOR DETAILS

EDWARD F. SINNOTT, LYLE SWIGER, AND PHILIP COLAVITA JR., DEL.

(Sheet 32)

Greenway

143

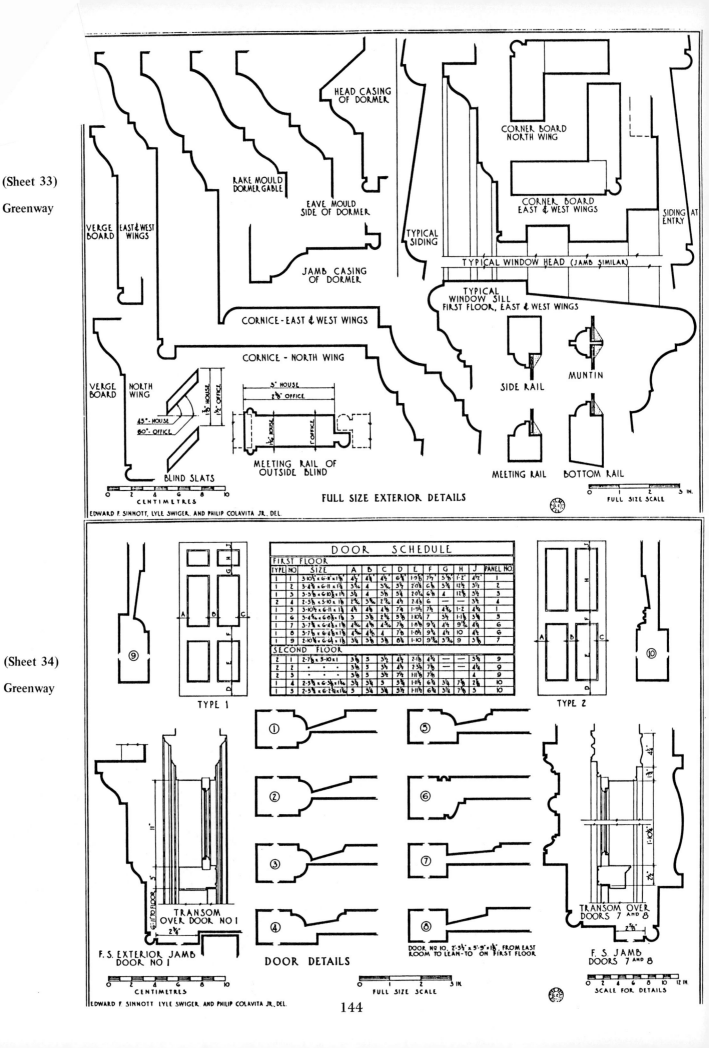

(Sheet 33)
Greenway

(Sheet 34)
Greenway

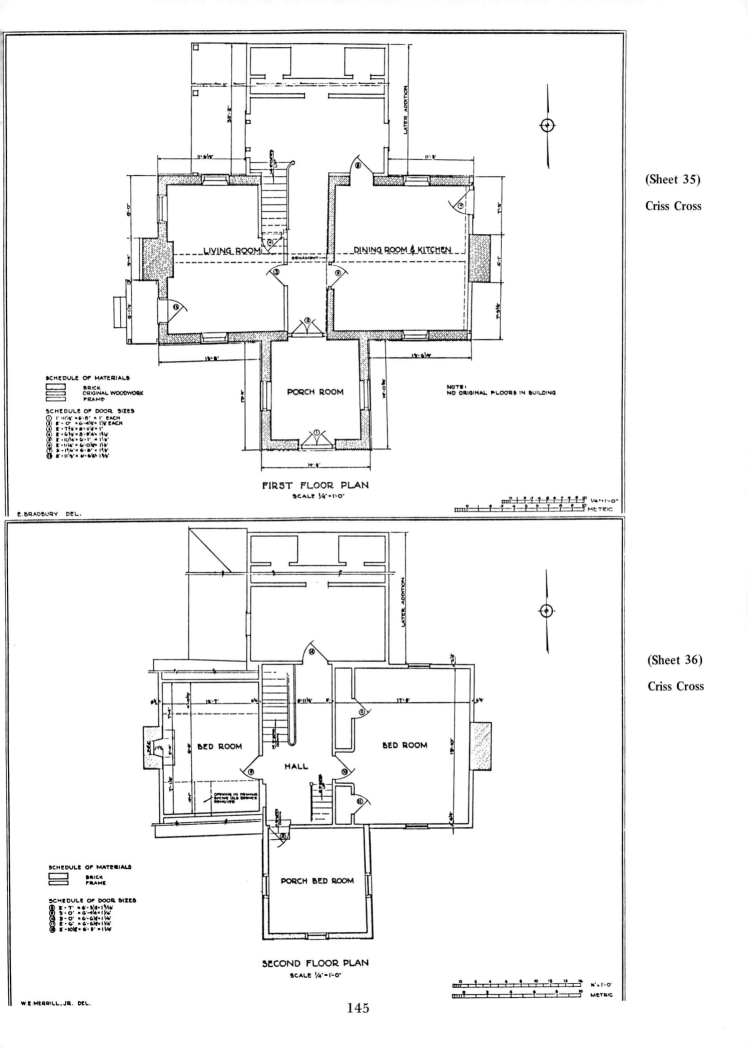

(Sheet 35)

Criss Cross

(Sheet 36)

Criss Cross

SCHEDULE OF MATERIALS

BRICK
ORIGINAL WOODWORK
FRAME·

SCHEDULE OF DOOR SIZES

LIVING ROOM

DINING ROOM & KITCHEN

ORNAMENT

PORCH ROOM

NOTE:
NO ORIGINAL FLOORS IN BUILDING

FIRST FLOOR PLAN
SCALE ¼" = 1'-0"

E. BRADBURY DEL.

BED ROOM

BED ROOM

HALL

OPENING IN FRAMING
SHOWS WAS FORMERLY
REMOVED

PORCH BED ROOM

SCHEDULE OF MATERIALS

BRICK
FRAME

SCHEDULE OF DOOR SIZES

SECOND FLOOR PLAN
SCALE ¼" = 1'-0"

W.E. MERRILL, JR. DEL.

145

NOTE:
ONLY ORIGINAL PORTIONS
OF BRICKWORK LINED IN

EAST ELEVATION
SCALE ¼" = 1'-0"

G.C. PYNE JR, DEL.

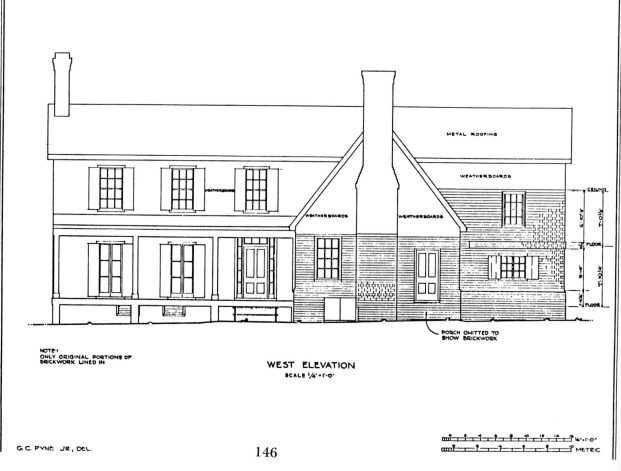

NOTE:
ONLY ORIGINAL PORTIONS OF
BRICKWORK LINED IN

WEST ELEVATION
SCALE ¼" = 1'-0"

PORCH OMITTED TO
SHOW BRICKWORK

G.C. PYNE JR, DEL.

146

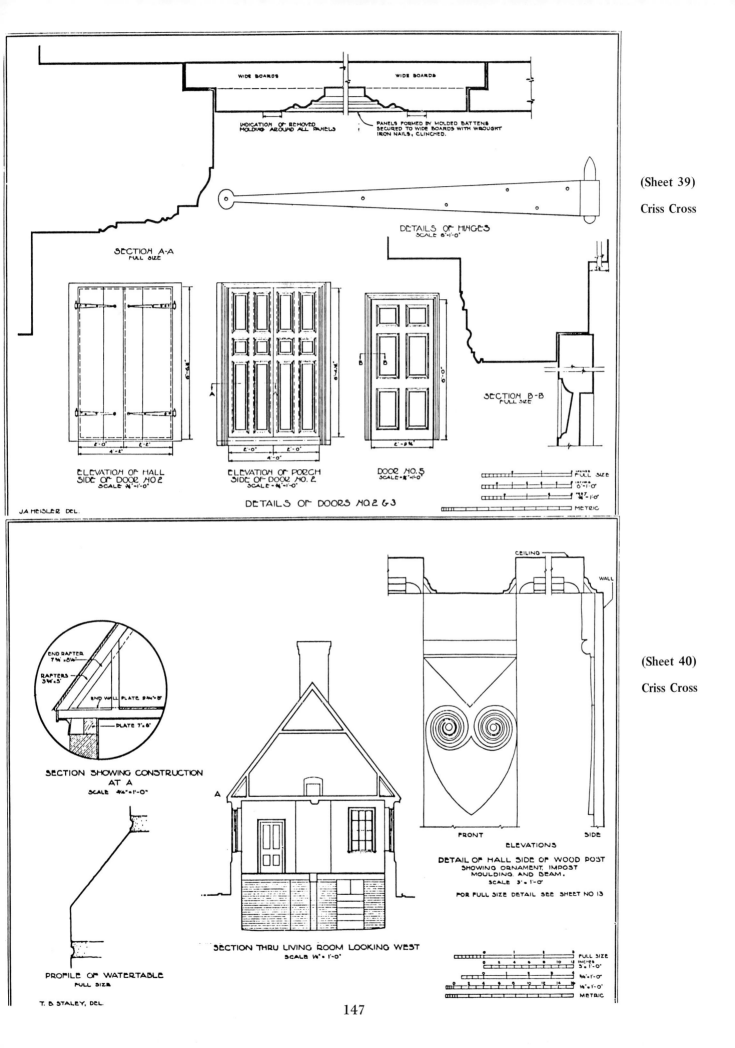

WIDE BOARDS   WIDE BOARDS

INDICATION OF REMOVED   PANELS FORMED BY MOLDED BATTENS
MOLDING AROUND ALL PANELS   SECURED TO WIDE BOARDS WITH WROUGHT
                               IRON NAILS, CLINCHED.

DETAILS OF HINGES
SCALE 6"=1'-0"

SECTION A-A
FULL SIZE

SECTION B-B
FULL SIZE

ELEVATION OF HALL   ELEVATION OF PORCH   DOOR NO.5
SIDE OF DOOR NO.2   SIDE OF DOOR NO.2   SCALE ⅜"=1'-0"
SCALE ¾"=1'-0"   SCALE ¾"=1'-0"

DETAILS OF DOORS NO.2 & 3

J.A. HEISLER DEL.

INCHES FULL SIZE
6"=1'-0"
1½"=1'-0"
METRIC

(Sheet 39)

Criss Cross

END RAFTER
7¾"x8¾"

RAFTERS
3¾"x5"

END WALL PLATE 8¾"x8"

PLATE 7"x8"

SECTION SHOWING CONSTRUCTION
AT A
SCALE 4½"=1'-0"

CEILING

WALL

FRONT   SIDE

ELEVATIONS

DETAIL OF HALL SIDE OF WOOD POST
SHOWING ORNAMENT, IMPOST
MOULDING, AND BEAM.
SCALE 3"=1'-0"

FOR FULL SIZE DETAIL SEE SHEET NO.13

SECTION THRU LIVING ROOM LOOKING WEST
SCALE ½"=1'-0"

PROFILE OF WATERTABLE
FULL SIZE

T. B. STALEY, DEL.

FULL SIZE
INCHES
3"=1'-0"
¾"=1'-0"
½"=1'-0"
METRIC

(Sheet 40)

Criss Cross

147

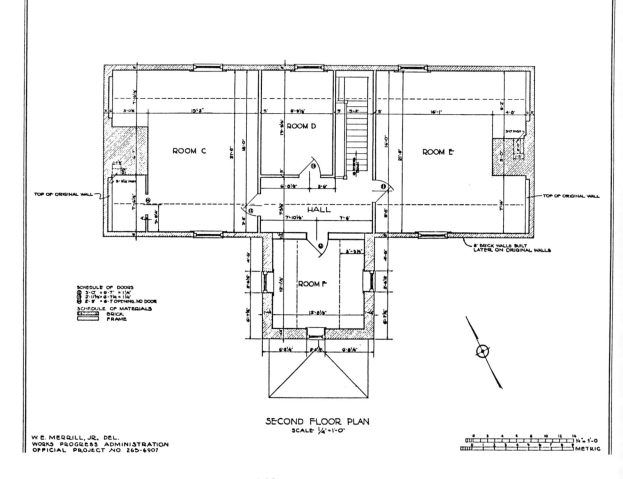

ONE STORY LATER FRAME ADDITION

ROOM A

HALL

ROOM B

ENTRY

SCHEDULE OF DOORS

SCHEDULE OF MATERIALS
BRICK
FRAME

PORCH LATER ADDITION

FIRST FLOOR PLAN
SCALE ¼" = 1'-0"

W.E. MERRILL JR. DEL.
WORKS PROGRESS ADMINISTRATION
OFFICIAL PROJECT NO. 265-6907

METRIC

ROOM C

ROOM D

ROOM E

TOP OF ORIGINAL WALL

HALL

TOP OF ORIGINAL WALL

8" BRICK WALLS BUILT
LATER ON ORIGINAL WALLS

ROOM F

SCHEDULE OF DOORS
SCHEDULE OF MATERIALS
BRICK
FRAME

SECOND FLOOR PLAN
SCALE ¼" = 1'-0"

W.E. MERRILL, JR. DEL.
WORKS PROGRESS ADMINISTRATION
OFFICIAL PROJECT NO. 265-6907

METRIC

148

NOTE: ONLY ORIGINAL BRICKWORK SHOWN HERE.

SOUTH ELEVATION
SCALE 1/4" = 1'-0"

W. E. MERRILL, JR. DEL.
WORKS PROGRESS ADMINISTRATION
OFFICIAL PROJECT NO. 265-6907

1/4"=1'-0"
METRIC

(Sheet 43)

Foster's Castle

NOTE: ONLY ORIGINAL BRICKWORK SHOWN HERE.

GABLE ENDS OF MAIN PORTION AND ELSEWHERE
BELOW WATERTABLE ALTERNATE FLEMISH AND
STRETCHER COURSES. ALL OTHER BRICKWORK
ABOVE WATERTABLE EXCEPT LATER FLEMISH
BOND. LATER BRICKWORK COMMON BOND.
BRICK SIZE— 8 1/2" x 2 3/4" x 4 1/4".

WEST ELEVATION
SCALE 1/4" = 1'-0"

W. E. MERRILL, JR. DEL.
WORKS PROGRESS ADMINISTRATION
OFFICIAL PROJECT NO. 265-6907

1/4"=1'-0"
METRIC

(Sheet 44)

Foster's Castle

(Sheet 45)

Foster's Castle

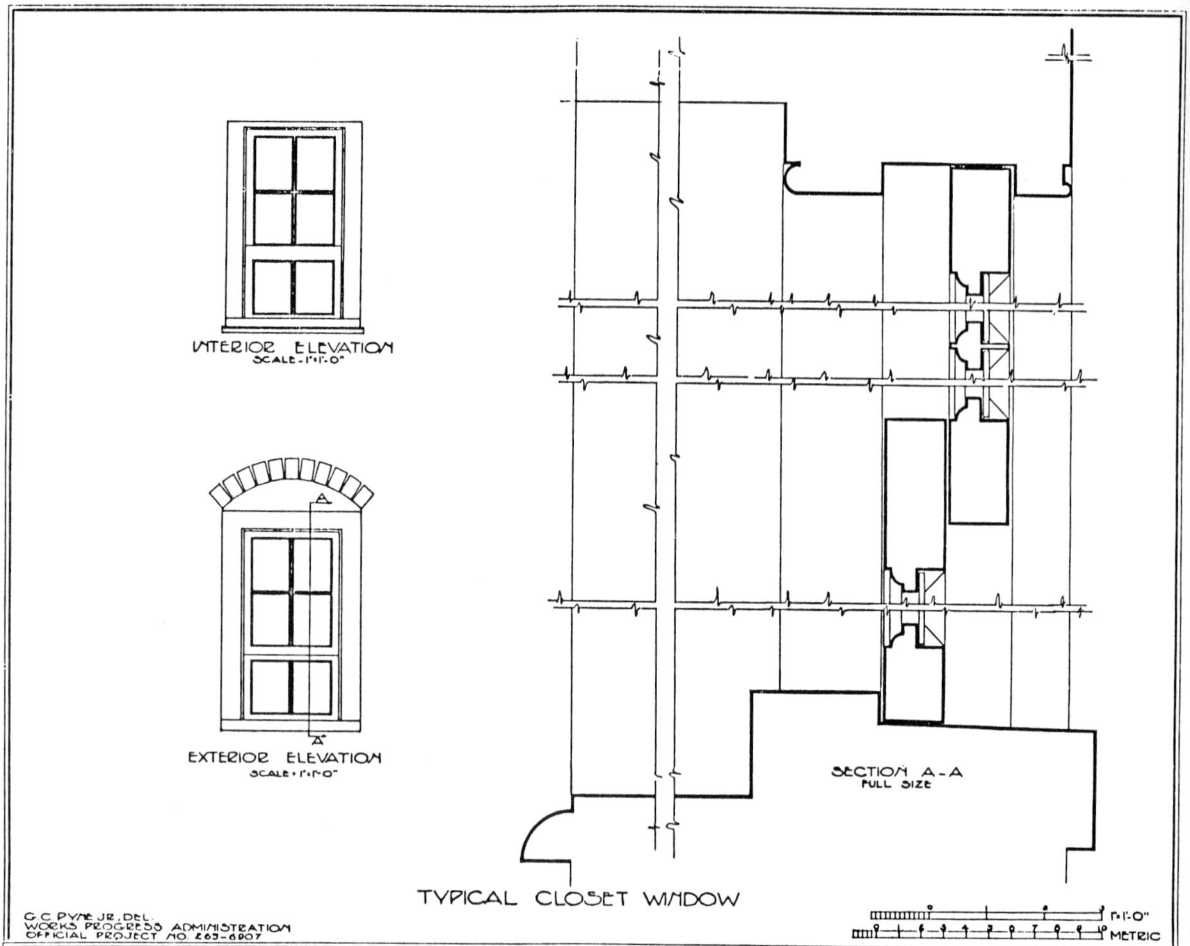

INTERIOR ELEVATION
SCALE 1"=1'-0"

EXTERIOR ELEVATION
SCALE 1"=1'-0"

SECTION A-A
FULL SIZE

TYPICAL CLOSET WINDOW

C.C. PYNE JR. DEL
WORKS PROGRESS ADMINISTRATION
OFFICIAL PROJECT NO. 265-6907

0   1'-0"
          METRIC

(Sheet 46)

Foster's Castle

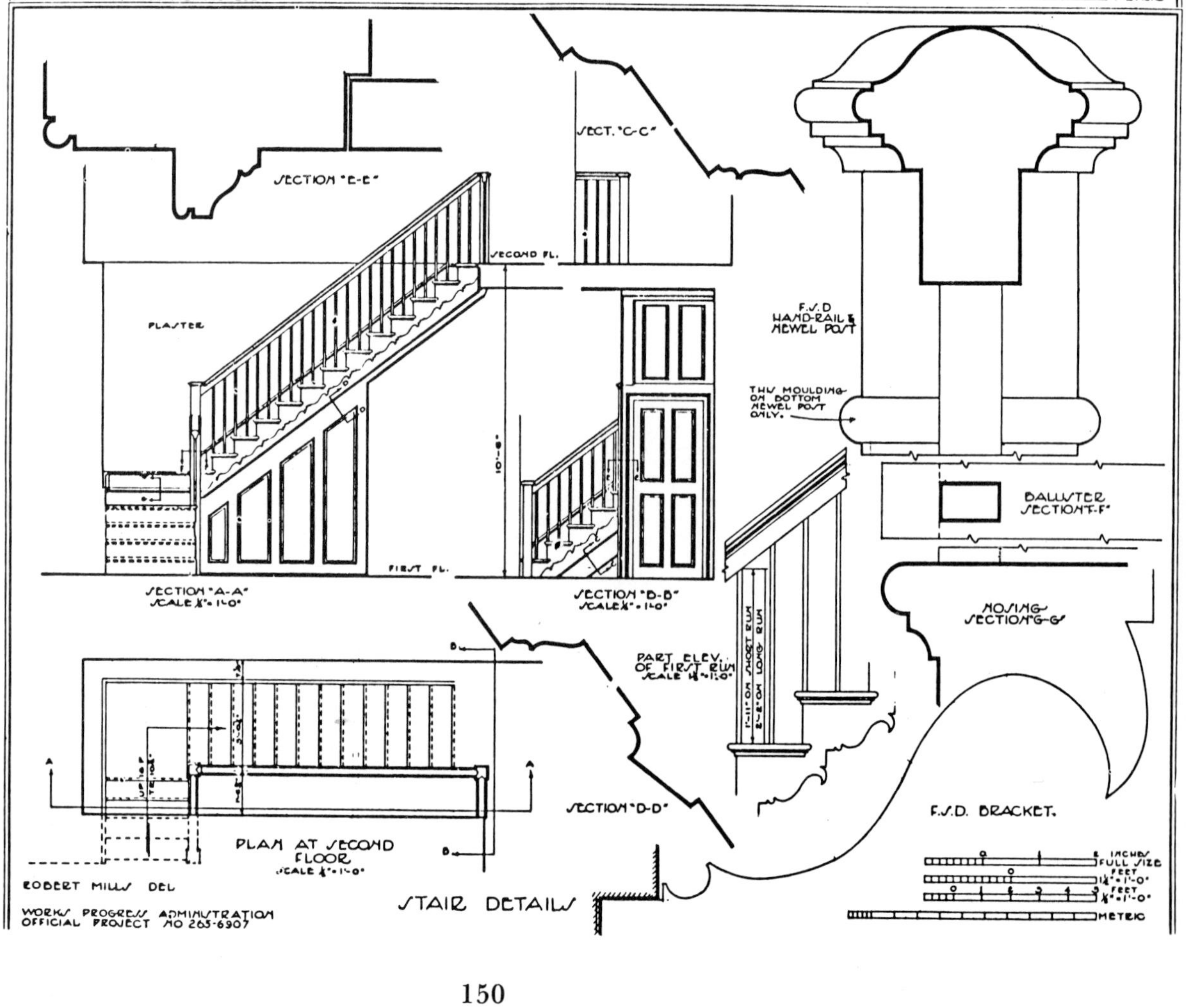

SECTION "E-E"

SECT. "C-C"

PLASTER

SECOND FL.

10'-8"

FIRST FL.

SECTION "A-A"
SCALE 1/2"=1'-0"

SECTION "D-D"
SCALE 1/2"=1'-0"

F.S.D.
HAND-RAIL &
NEWEL POST

THIS MOULDING
ON BOTTOM
NEWEL POST
ONLY.

BALUSTER
SECTION "F"

NOSING
SECTION "G"

PART ELEV.
OF FIRST RUN
SCALE 1½"=1'-0"

SECTION "D-D"

STAIR DETAILS

F.S.D. BRACKET.

PLAN AT SECOND
FLOOR
SCALE 1/2"=1'-0"

ROBERT MILLS DEL
WORKS PROGRESS ADMINISTRATION
OFFICIAL PROJECT NO 265-6907

6 INCHES
FULL SIZE
FEET
1½"=1'-0"
FEET
½"=1'-0"
METRIC

150

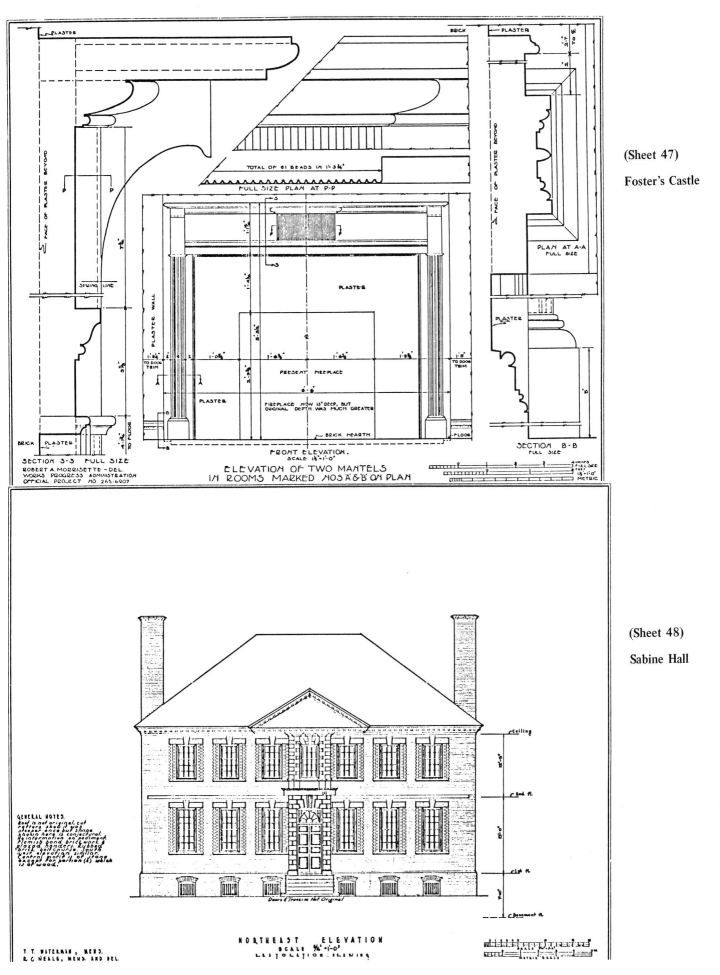

151

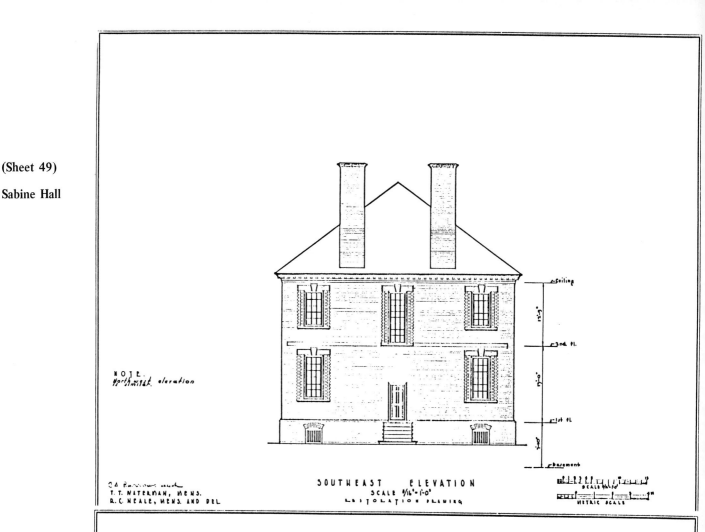

(Sheet 49)

Sabine Hall

NOTE.
North-with elevation

T. T. WATERMAN, MEAS.
R. C. NEALE, MEAS. AND DEL.

SOUTHEAST ELEVATION
SCALE 9/16"=1'-0"
RESTORATION FRAMING

METRIC SCALE

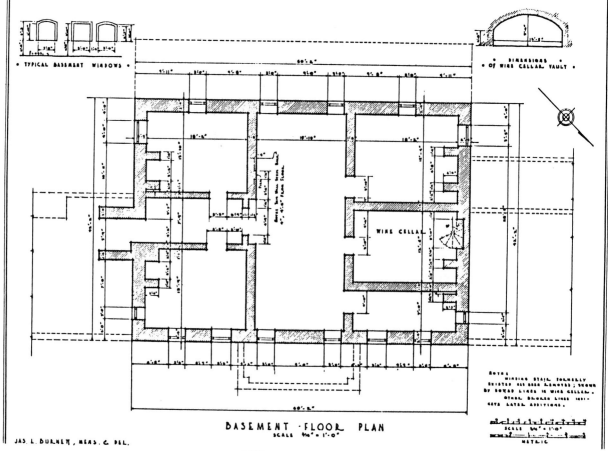

(Sheet 50)

Sabine Hall

TYPICAL BASEMENT WINDOWS

DIMENSIONS
OF WINE CELLAR VAULT

WINE CELLAR

NOTE:
WINDING STAIR FORMERLY
EXISTED AS HERE REMOVED; SHOWN
BY BROAD LINES IN WINE CELLAR.
OTHER BROKEN LINES INDI-
CATE LATER ADDITIONS.

JAS. L. BURNETT, MEAS. & DEL.

BASEMENT FLOOR PLAN
SCALE 3/16"=1'-0"

METRIC

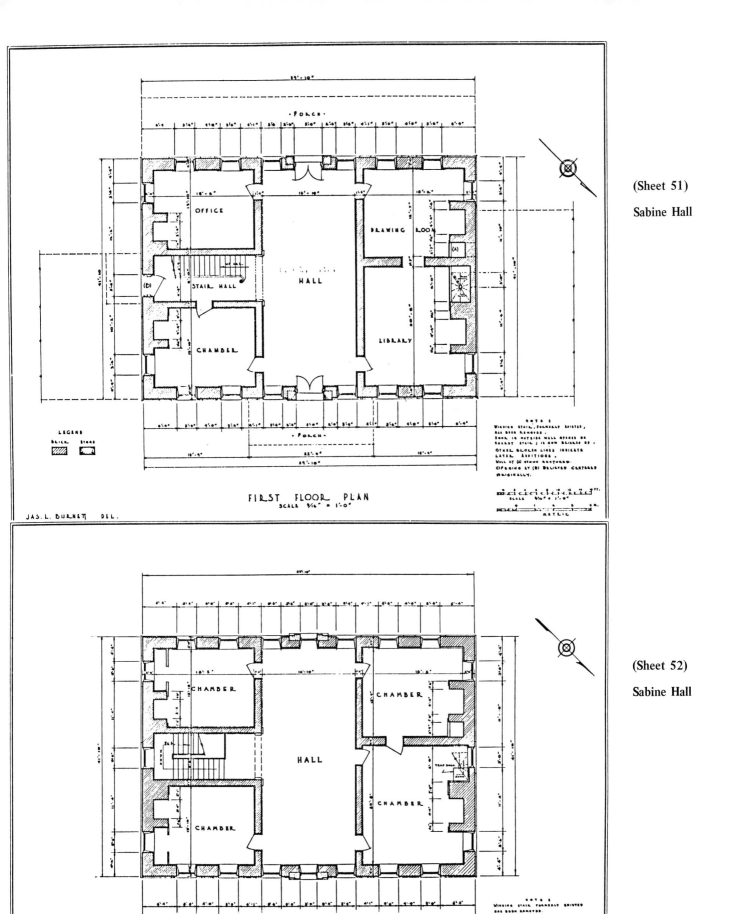

FIRST FLOOR PLAN
SCALE 3/16" = 1'-0"

JAS. L. BURNETT DEL.

LEGEND
BRICK   STONE

(Sheet 51)

Sabine Hall

SECOND FLOOR PLAN
SCALE 3/16" = 1'-0"

H.J. FURMAN-DEL.

LEGEND
STONE
BRICK

(Sheet 52)

Sabine Hall

153

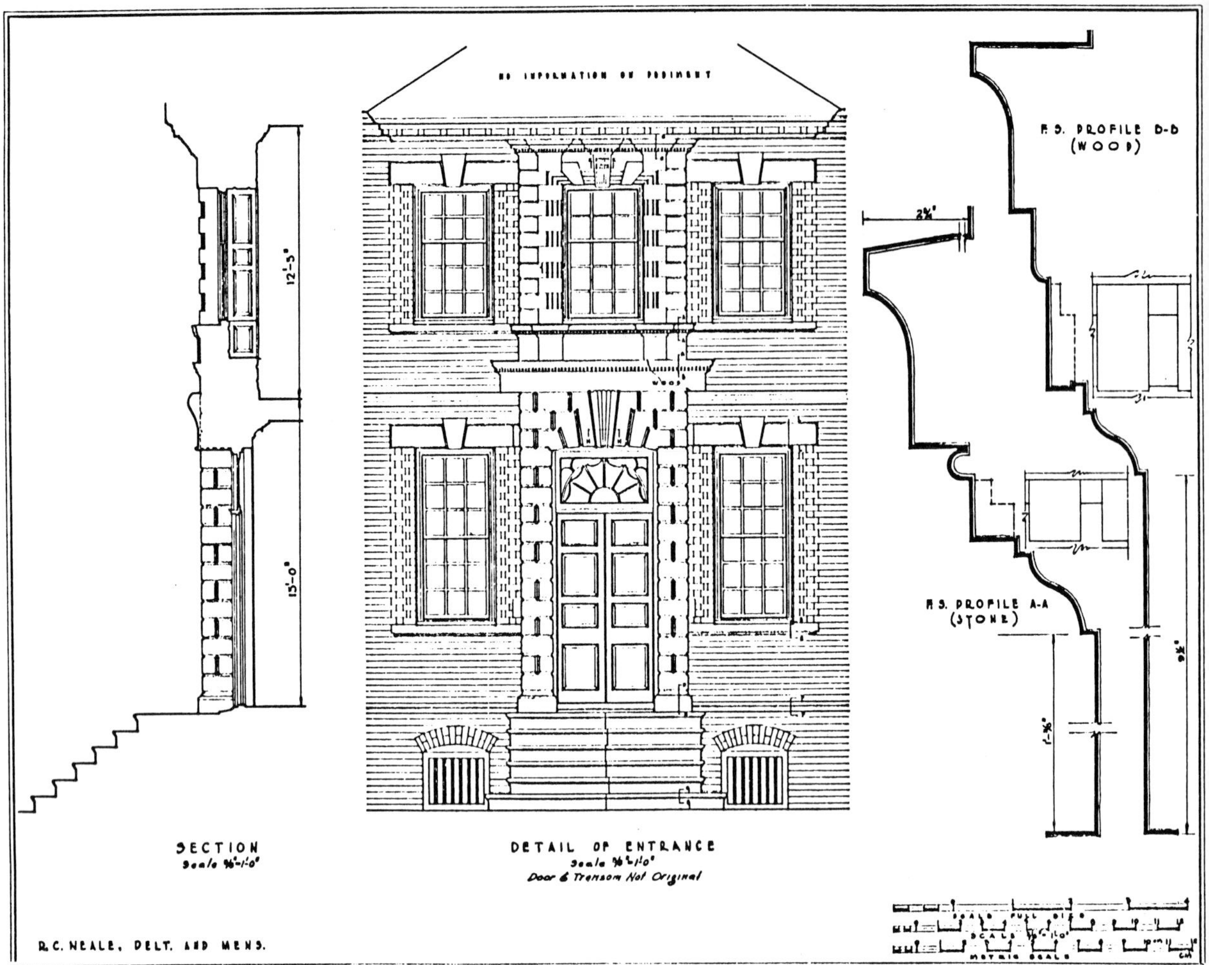

NO INFORMATION OF PEDIMENT

F.S. PROFILE D-D
(WOOD)

WOOD

F.S. PROFILE A-A
(STONE)

SECTION
Scale ⅜"=1'-0"

DETAIL OF ENTRANCE
Scale ⅜"=1'-0"
Door & Transom Not Original

R.C. NEALE, DELT. AND MENS.

F.S. PROFILE OF
WALL PANEL

WOOD
PLASTER

F.S. PROFILE OF
CHAIR RAIL

F.S. PROFILE OF
PANEL IN WINDOW JAMB

EAST ELEVATION OF SECOND FLOOR HALL
Scale ½"=1'-0"

F.S. PROFILE OF DOOR TRIM

WOOD

PLASTER

WOOD

PLASTER

NORTH ELEVATION OF SECOND FLOOR HALL
Scale ½"=1'-0"

W.T. RAMSAY DELT. AND MENS.

154

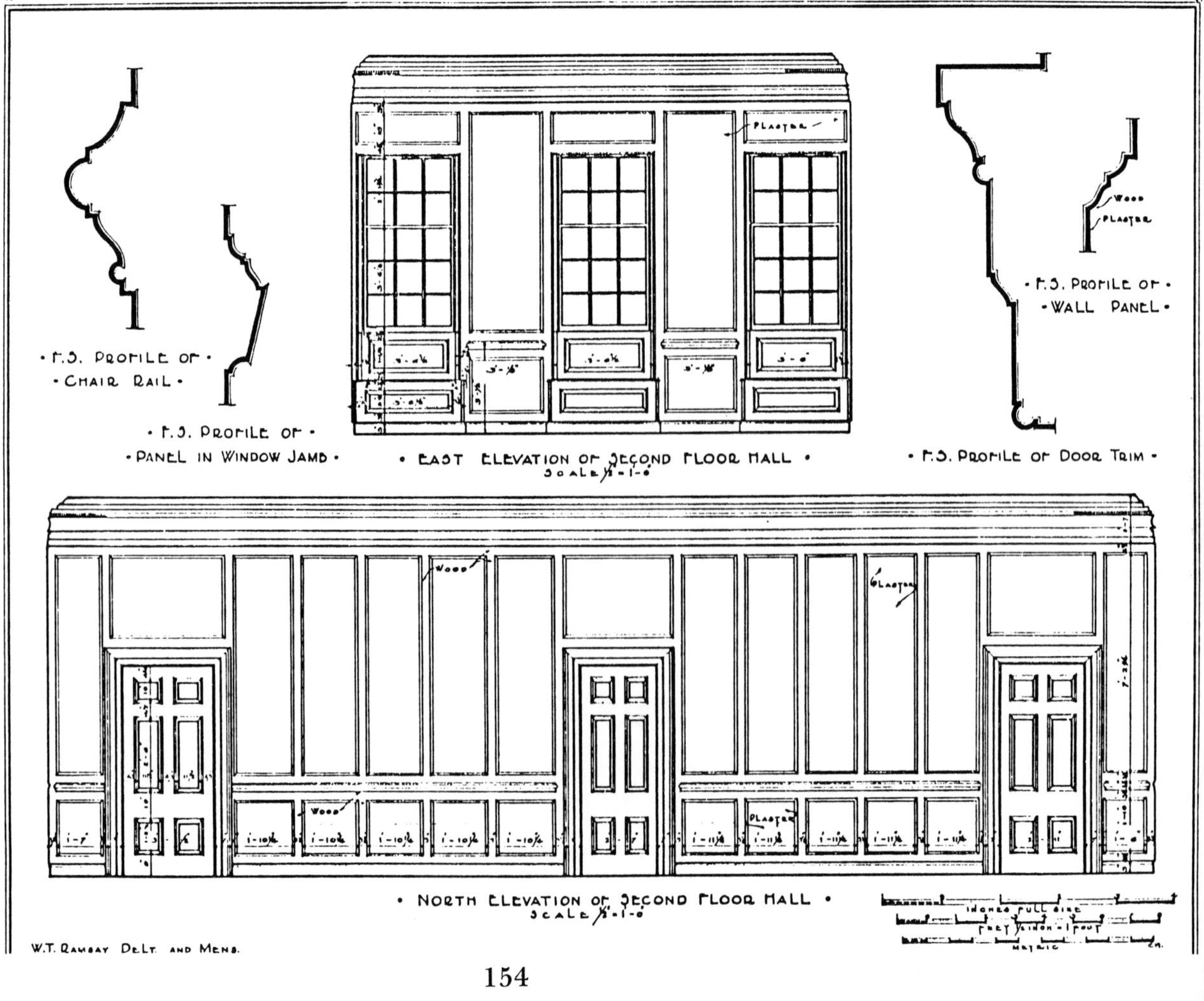

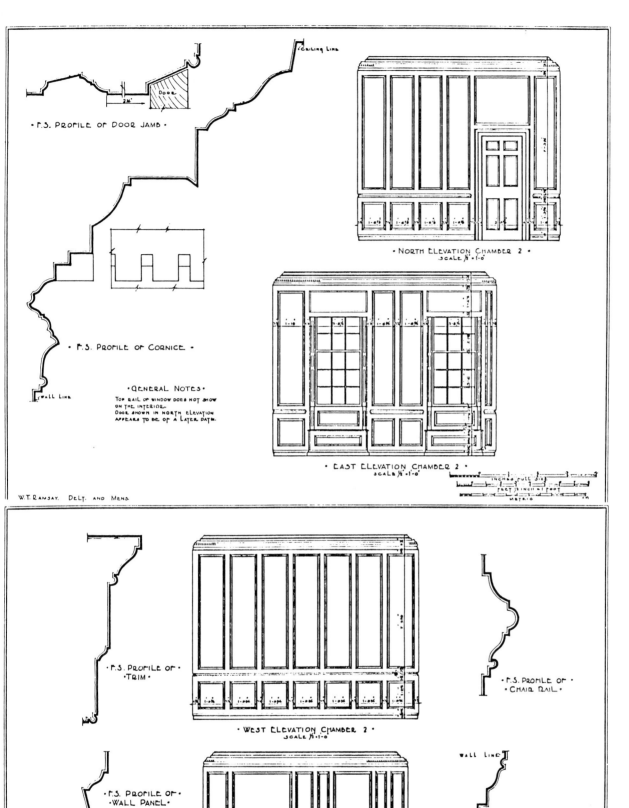

· F.S. PROFILE OF DOOR JAMB ·

· F.S. PROFILE OF CORNICE ·

·GENERAL NOTES·

TOP RAIL OF WINDOW DOES NOT SHOW
ON THE INTERIOR.
DOOR SHOWN IN NORTH ELEVATION
APPEARS TO BE OF A LATER DATE.

· NORTH ELEVATION CHAMBER 2 ·
SCALE ½" = 1'-0"

· EAST ELEVATION CHAMBER 2 ·
SCALE ½" = 1'-0"

W.T. RAMSAY. DELT. AND MENS.

(Sheet 55)

Sabine Hall

·F.S. PROFILE OF·
·TRIM·

·F.S. PROFILE OF·
·WALL PANEL·

·GENERAL NOTES·

DOOR IN SOUTH ELEVATION HAS BEEN
REMOVED.
ORIGINAL MANTEL HAS BEEN REMOVED.

· WEST ELEVATION CHAMBER 2 ·
SCALE ½" = 1'-0"

· SOUTH ELEVATION CHAMBER 2 ·
SCALE ½" = 1'-0"

·F.S. PROFILE OF·
·CHAIR RAIL·

WALL LINE

·F.S. PROFILE OF·
·BASE BOARD·

FLOOR LINE

(Sheet 56)

Sabine Hall

W.T. RAMSAY. DELT. AND MENS.

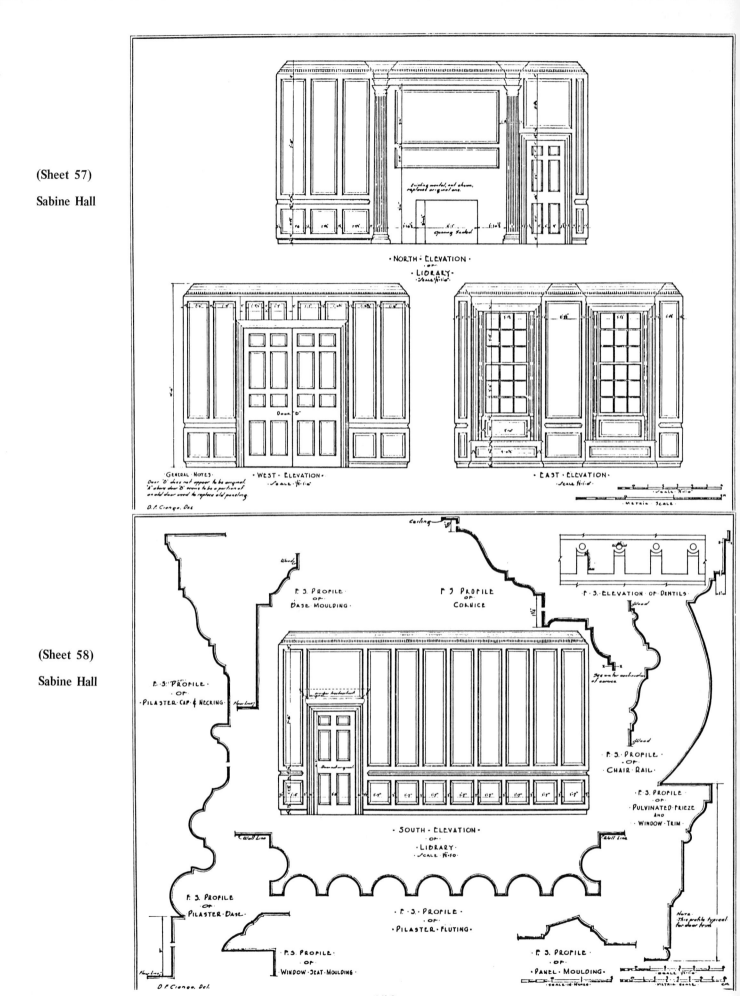

(Sheet 57)

Sabine Hall

(Sheet 58)

Sabine Hall

156

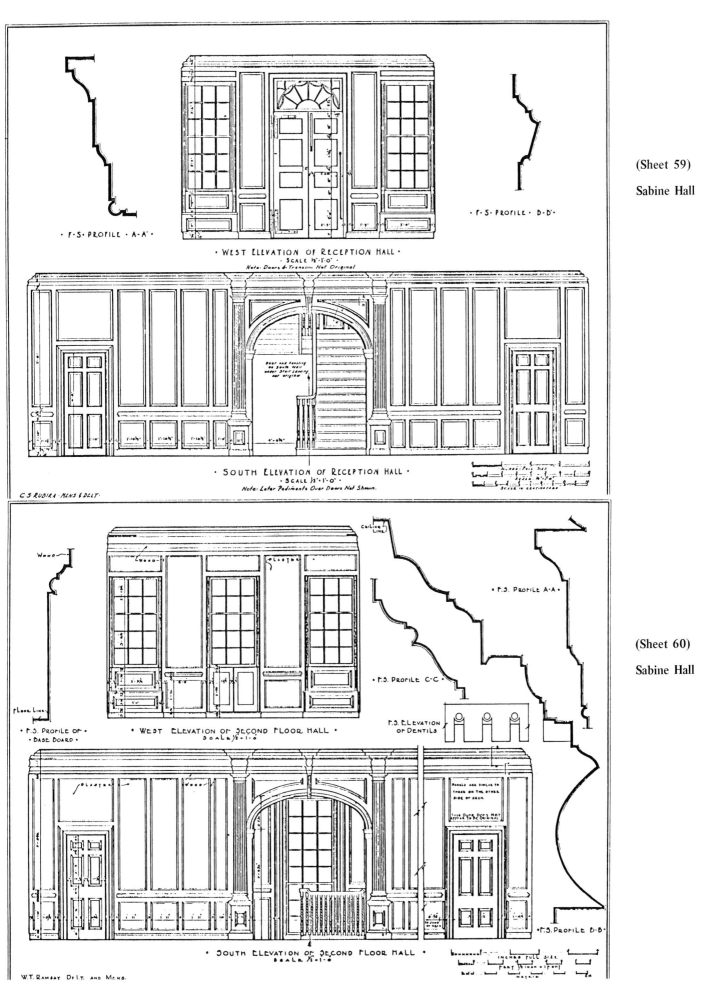

· F·S· PROFILE · A-A' ·

· F·S· PROFILE · D-D' ·

· WEST ELEVATION OF RECEPTION HALL ·
· SCALE ½'·1'·0" ·
Note: Doors & Transom Not Original

· SOUTH ELEVATION OF RECEPTION HALL ·
· SCALE ½'·1'·0" ·
Note: Later Pediments Over Doors Not Shown.

C S RUDIRA · MENS & DELT ·

SCALE IN CENTIMETERS

(Sheet 59)

Sabine Hall

· F·S· PROFILE A·A ·

· F·S· PROFILE C-C ·

· F·S· ELEVATION OF DENTILS ·

· F·S· PROFILE OF ·
· BASE BOARD ·

· WEST ELEVATION OF SECOND FLOOR HALL ·
· SCALE ½'·1'·0" ·

PANELS ARE SIMILAR TO THOSE ON THE OTHER SIDE OF ARCH.

THIS DOOR DOES NOT APPEAR TO BE ORIGINAL

· SOUTH ELEVATION OF SECOND FLOOR HALL ·
· SCALE ½'·1'·0" ·

· F·S· PROFILE D·B ·

INCHES FULL SIZE.
FEET SCALE ½ INCH · 1 FOOT

W.T. RAMSAY DELT. AND MENS.

(Sheet 60)

Sabine Hall

157

(Sheet 61)

Sabine Hall

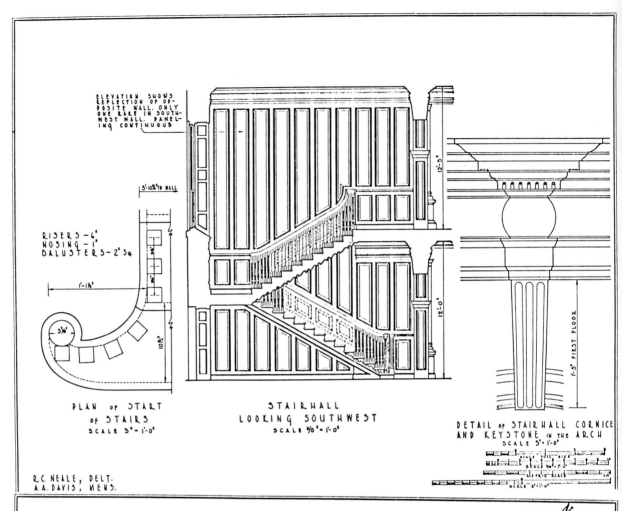

ELEVATION SHOWS
REFLECTION OF OP-
POSITE WALL. ONLY
ONE RAKE IN SOUTH-
WEST WALL. PANEL-
ING CONTINUOUS

12'-5"

3'-10½"TO WALL

RISERS-6'
NOSING-1'
BALUSTERS-2" Sq.

12'-0"

1'-1½"

5½"

10½"

1'-5" FIRST FLOOR

PLAN OF START
OF STAIRS
SCALE 3"=1'-0"

STAIRHALL
LOOKING SOUTHWEST
SCALE 4/0"=1'-0"

DETAIL OF STAIRHALL CORNICE
AND KEYSTONE IN THE ARCH
SCALE 3"=1'-0"

R.C. NEALE, DELT.
A.A. DAVIS, MEAS.

(Sheet 62)

Sabine Hall

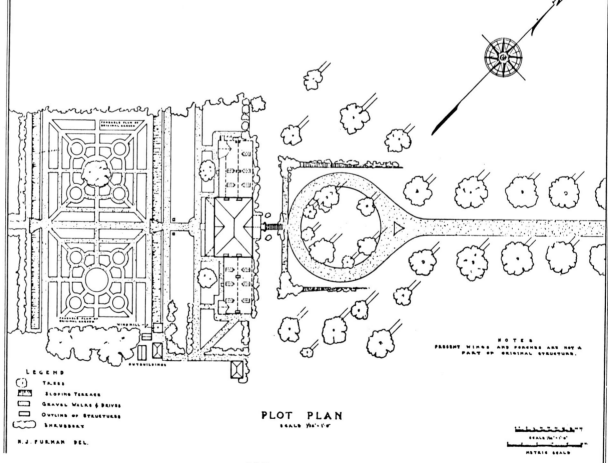

N

NOTES
PRESENT WINGS AND PORCHES ARE NOT A
PART OF ORIGINAL STRUCTURE.

LEGEND
○ TREES
SLOPING TERRACE
GRAVEL WALKS & DRIVES
OUTLINE OF STRUCTURES
SHRUBBERY

PLOT PLAN
SCALE ⅛"=1'-0"

SCALE ⅛"=1'-0"
METRIC SCALE

R.J. FURMAN DEL.

158

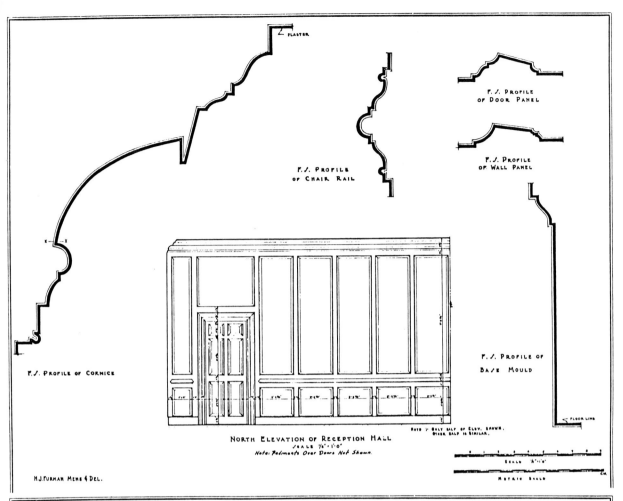

F. S. PROFILE
OF DOOR PANEL

F. S. PROFILE
of CHAIR RAIL

F. S. PROFILE
OF WALL PANEL

(Sheet 63)

Sabine Hall

F. S. PROFILE OF
BASE MOULD

F. S. PROFILE OF CORNICE

NORTH ELEVATION OF RECEPTION HALL
SCALE ⅛" = 1'-0"
Note: Pediments Over Doors Not Shown.

Note: Only Half of Elev. Shown.
Other Half is Similar.

SCALE ⅛" = 1'-0"

METRIC SCALE

H. J. FURMAN MENS & DEL.

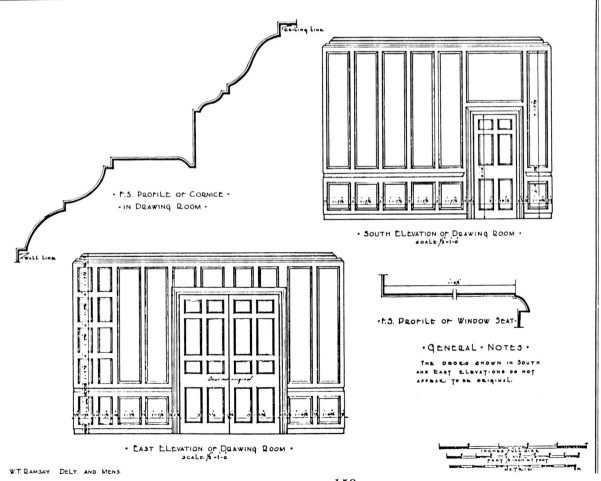

· F. S. PROFILE OF CORNICE ·
· IN DRAWING ROOM ·

· SOUTH ELEVATION OF DRAWING ROOM ·
SCALE ⅛" = 1'-0"

(Sheet 64)

Sabine Hall

· F. S. PROFILE OF WINDOW SEAT ·

· GENERAL · NOTES ·

THE DOORS SHOWN IN SOUTH
AND EAST ELEVATIONS DO NOT
APPEAR TO BE ORIGINAL.

· EAST ELEVATION OF DRAWING ROOM ·
SCALE ⅛" = 1'-0"

W. T. RAMSAY DELT. AND MENS.

WALL LINE

F.S. PROFILE OF BASE BOARD

FLOOR LINE

WEST ELEVATION OF DRAWING ROOM
SCALE ½=1-0

WALL LINE

F.S. PROFILE OF CHAIR RAIL

F.S. PROFILE OF PANEL A

·GENERAL NOTES·

PANEL A APPEARS AROUND CHIMNEY
BREAST AND IS LATER THAN PANEL B.
ORIGINAL MANTEL HAS BEEN REMOVED.
WINDOW SASH ARE NOT ORIGINAL.
DOOR SHOWN IN NORTH ELEVATION
IS OF A LATER DATE.

SIDE ELEVATION OF
CHIMNEY BREAST
SCALE ½=1-0

NORTH ELEVATION OF DRAWING ROOM
SCALE ½=1-0

F.S. PROFILE OF PANEL B

INCHES FULL SIZE
FEET ½ INCH=1 FOOT
METRIC

W.T. RAMSAY, DELT. AND MENS.

160

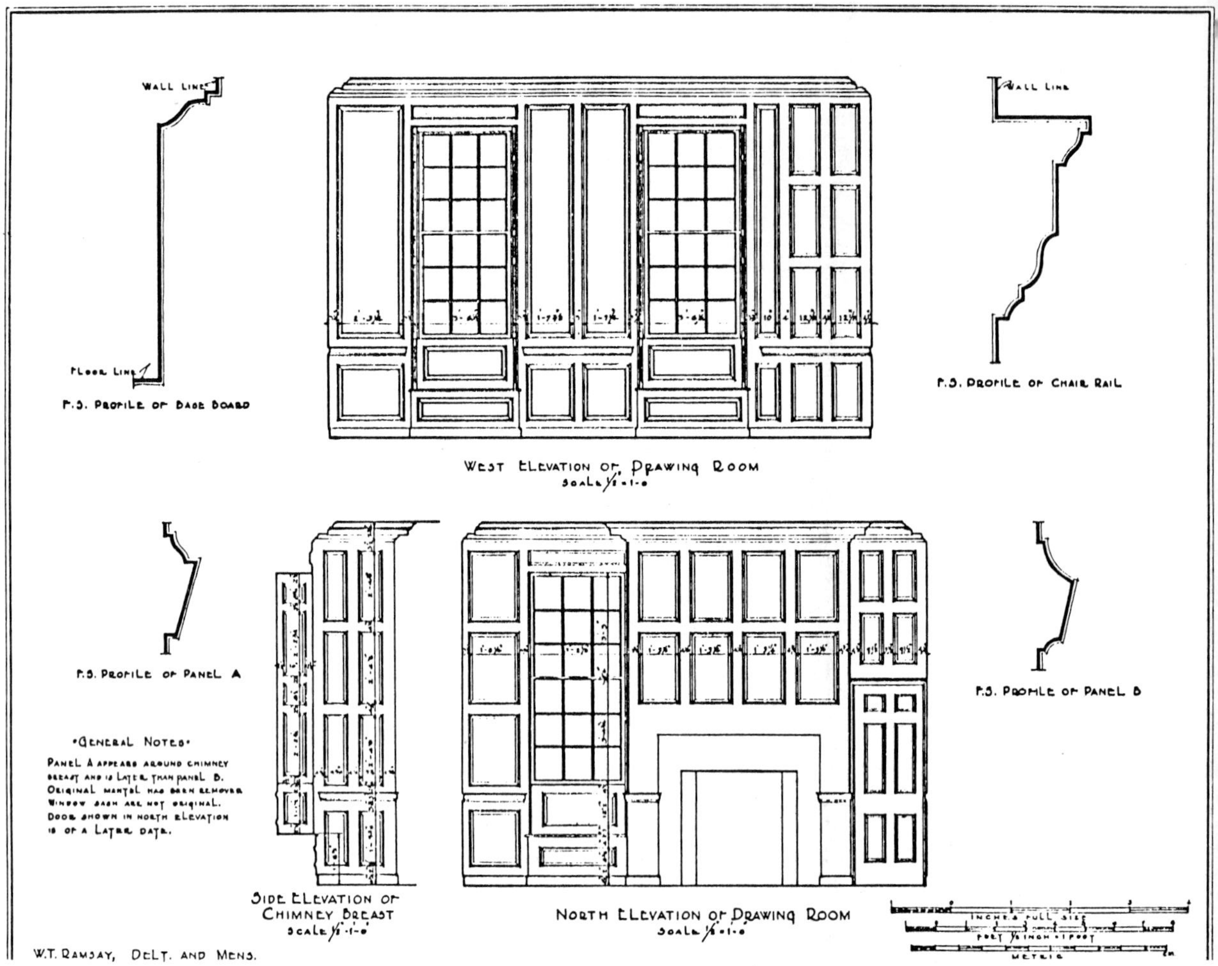